IN ITALY

Writers

Giorgio Chiosso
Mariolina Meliodà Freeth
David Waugh
Henry Pluckrose
Caroline Rainger

Edited by

Picot Cassidy

Designed by

Wendi Watson

Cartoons by

David Lock

Illustrations and maps by

Alan Suttie
Donald Myall
Caroline Rainger
David Lagrange

EMC/Paradigm Publishing, Saint Paul, Minnesota

About this book

In Italy gives a wide variety of practical Italian phrases that help readers to cope with everyday situations. Where possible, authentic material is included to bring Italy and things Italian to life.

☆☆☆☆

In the book, look out for:

Come si dice?

This section gives key vocabulary and phrases to help the reader in practical situations, such as ordering food and drinks, asking directions, and sending postcards. The title means 'How do you say it?' English equivalents of the Italian words and phrases are given, unless the meaning of the Italian is clear from the context. English subtitles appear under the cartoons.

Lo sapevate...? means 'Do you know..?' and this section highlights short items of interesting information.

Da non perdere! In English this means 'Don't miss it!' This section provides information on places, people or points of interest that readers should look out for when they are in Italy.

As well as in **Come si dice?**, Italian words and phrases appear throughout the text of the book. Italian words and phrases are usually indicated in bold type with the English equivalent following.

The names of cities or regions are also given in Italian to accustom readers to the Italian version. Where these names appear for the first time in the book the English equivalents are also given. Original Italian place names which are the same as in English do not appear in bold type.

Where Latin or Greek words or other foreign words that differ from English appear, they are shown in italic type.

☆☆☆☆

How to say it in Italian

At the back of the book is a pronunciation guide. There is also a short introduction to some points of Italian grammar. This includes a brief summary of the grammar of the definite article, noun endings in singular and plural, and adjectives.

Speak up!

– Generally, the formal, polite **Lei** verb form is given in phrases. Occasionally, the informal **tu** form has been included. If you're not sure which to use, try the polite form.
– Don't be shy about speaking Italian. You'll find that Italians are usually happy to help you try to speak Italian.
– When you meet people, remember to say:

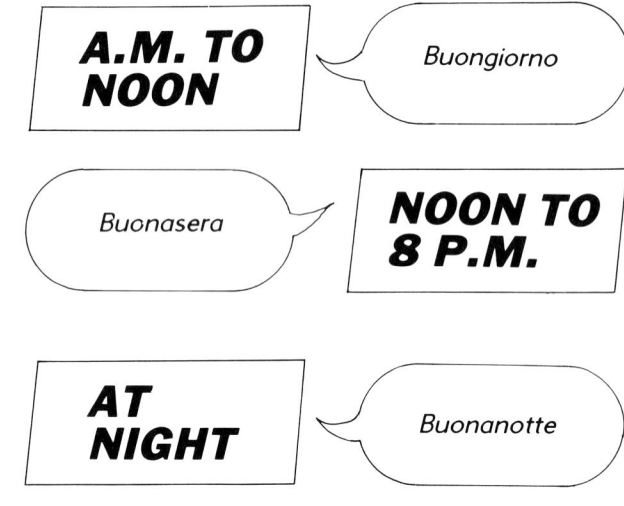

– If you don't understand what someone is saying, just say politely:

© Chancerel Publishers Ltd. 1988

Reprinted 1998

All rights reserved. No part of this publication may be reproduced, recorded, transmitted or stored in any retrieval system, in any form whatsoever, without the written permission of the copyright holders.

ISBN 0-8219-0480-9
Catalog no. 55265

Published by:
EMC/Paradigm Publishing
875 Montreal Way
Saint Paul,
Minnesota 55102, USA

Produced by:
Chancerel International
Publishers Ltd.
120 Long Acre
London WC2E 9PA
United Kingdom

Graphic reproduction by:
Times Graphics, Singapore
Technic Color Separation, Hong Kong

Printed in Hong Kong

Contents

Photographs

Ancient Art and Architecture 19, 44; Architectural Association 24; Associated Press 7; Antony Blake 58; Azienda Agraria LISINI 27; British Olivetti Ltd. 28; Picot Cassidy 11, 32 (2), 35 (6), 36, 59, 62, 69; Chancerel/J. Chipps 34, 35, 64, 69, 70, 75, 76, 79; Chancerel/B. Hallmann 13, 15, 30, 32, 33, 40, 41, 42, 45, 55 (2), 57, 62, 70; CIS 58; ENIT (Italian State Tourist Office) London 4, 5, 6, 7, 8 (3), 9, 10 (3), 12, 16, 24 (2), 27, 34 (2), 36 (2), 38 (2), 38, 41 (2), 52, 53, 67 (2), 71; Leo Fasolato 71; Fiat 28; GEC-Marconi 78; Lillian Gordon 79; Guardian/E. Hamilton-West 77; Mansell Collection 13, 14, 15 (3), 17 (3), 19, 20, 22 (3), 23, 46, 51 (3), 52, 56, 57; Maserati 29; Montessori Organisation 78 (2); National Gallery 21; Navigazione Lago di Como 78; Olivetti 28, 29 (3); Polenghi 60 (3); Scala 16, 45, 46, 49, 50; Joachim Schulz 47; David Simson/Das Photo 4, 5, 8, 9 (2), 10 (2), 11 (2), 15, 19, 21, 22, 23 (3), 24 (2), 25 (2), 26 (5), 27 (3), 29 (4), 30 (4), 31 (2), 36, 37 (5), 38 (6), 40 (3), 41 (3), 42 (5), 43, 44 (4), 45 (3), 46, 47 (5), 48 (4), 49 (5), 50, 51 (2), 52 (2), 53 (2), 54 (5), 55 (2), 56 (4), 57, 58, 59 (2), 61, 62 (3), 63 (2), 64 (3), 65 (11), 66 (5), 67 (2), 68 (4), 69 (2), 71 (3), 72 (3), 73 (3), 74, 75 (4), 77 (2), 79; Sporting Pictures 34, 72; The Magic of Italy 38; Victoria and Albert Museum 18, 19; Villas Italia 37, 41; Mike Watson 56, 57; Wedgwood 12.

Every effort has been made to contact the copyright holders of all illustrations. The publishers apologize for any omissions and will be pleased to make the necessary arrangements at the first opportunity.

Viva l'italiano!

The word **italiano** can mean several things—the Italian language, an Italian person or something Italian. **L'italiano**, the Italian language, has existed far longer than Italy! Until 1870, the Italian peninsula consisted of separate states, ruled by local princes, or foreign powers, such as Austria and Spain, who insisted on the use of their own languages. Only after the fight for Italian independence was won in 1870 did a single Italian state, with its capital in Rome, come into being. For the first time it had a common official language—**l'italiano**.

Carta d'identità

Name: Italian

Date of birth: at least seven centuries ago.

Place of birth: Tuscany.

Presently spoken in: Italian peninsula, Sicily, Sardinia, southern Switzerland (mainly in the canton of Ticino).

Spoken by: in Italy more than 57 million people. Italian is regarded by millions more around the world (particularly in the USA and Australia) as part of their cultural inheritance, although they might not all speak Italian.

TUSCANY WHERE THE ITALIAN LANGUAGE WAS BORN.

What is Italian?

Italian was originally a dialect spoken in the city of **Firenze** (Florence) and its surrounding region of **la Toscana** (Tuscany). This dialect had developed from Latin, the language of the ancient Romans. There were two versions of Latin: an official kind used by the Catholic Church and for official documents; and another everyday language spoken by the people. The everyday Latin was called vulgar Latin from the Latin word *vulgus* meaning common people.

An official Latin writer would have referred to a horse as *equus*, while the people called it *caballus*. In Florentine dialect, and later in modern Italian, this word became **cavallo**.

*The great poet, Dante Alighieri (1265–1321), known as the father of the Italian language, was born in **Firenze**. His best known work, **La Divina Commedia** (The Divine Comedy), was written in the new language that the people of **la Toscana**, were beginning to speak instead of vulgar Latin. This was the first time that Italian had been used in a work of literature.*

Dante Alighieri

Some 40,000 English words come from Latin roots, so there are sometimes similarities between Latin, Italian and English words:

Latin	Italian	English
Rosa	Rosa	Rose
Poeta	Poeta	Poet
Vasum	Vaso	Vase
Musica	Musica	Music
Classis	Classe	Class

Pulmonary* infection? Ah sì! Infezione polmonare.

Pulmonary? What's that?

* pulmonary = connected with the lungs, from Latin *pulmo* (lung). The Italian word for lung is **polmone**.

Because many more Italian words than English ones are closely linked to their Latin roots, it is often easy for Italians to understand medical and scientific terminology in English. English medical and scientific terms are often words of Latin origin rather than their more simple common equivalents.

Sounds Italian?

You may know more Italian than you think, as we use a number of Italian words in English. Most people probably know that words like **spaghetti**, **pizza**, or **ciao** are originally Italian. What about the words below? Study the pronunciation guide inside the back cover and try saying these words the Italian way.

SCENARIO **PICCOLO** **CONFETTI**
RIVIERA **GALA**
MALARIA **PIANO**
TROMBONE **INCOGNITO** **VILLA**

Sign language—Italian style

Italians often express themselves with their hands, as well as with words. They have gestures to show they're surprised, curious, or angry.

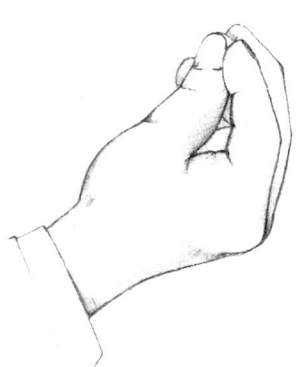

One of the most typical gestures is made with the hand turned palm side up and the tips of the fingers pressed against the thumb. This gesture is usually connected with questioning something emphatically. Once particularly associated with i napoletani (people from Naples), it is now used all over Italy.

In another gesture, often used to tell off naughty children, the hand is held palm side up and with the fingers together.

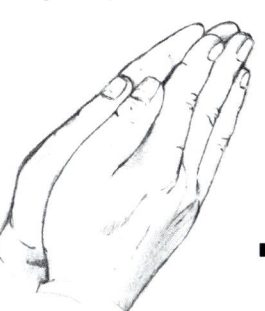
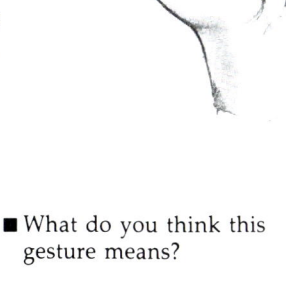

■ What do you think this gesture means?

Dialetti

Although there is an official version of Italian, many regional **dialetti** (dialects) exist. These dialects originated from the fusion of local languages with the languages spoken by the people who invaded Italy. Even within a single region, there are local variations on the main regional **dialetto**. With the improvement of mass communications and education in the 20th century, people who were only able to speak in their local dialect also began to learn standard Italian. There are still some regions where people speak **un dialetto** at home.

In the northwest of Italy, many French invasions over the centuries have influenced local dialects. These often sound closer to French than Italian. In some areas, French is spoken as well as Italian.

The Austrians brought German to the northeast. In the German-speaking areas in the **Trentino-Alto Adige** region, the proportion of German speakers to Italian speakers is two to one.

In southern Italy over the centuries, the Greeks, Arabs and Spaniards, who came as conquerors, left traces of their languages. The Italian words for artichoke (**il carciofo**) and apricot (**l'albicocca**) come from Arabic.

A German-language inn sign from Bolzano, Alto Adige.

Lo sapevate . . . ?

✳ A boy is called . . .

un bambino in standard Italian.

un fiöl (ö pronounced as 'er') in **Torino** (Turin).

un guaglione in **Napoli** (Naples).

un toso in **Venezia** (Venice).

✳ **Spaghetti** is plural, because it means a collection of **spaghetto** (strands of pasta). An Italian would say **spaghetto**, if s/he was referring to an individual strand, but **spaghetti** if s/he was talking about a plateful.

All the other kinds of pasta are also plural, because you usually have more than one piece on your plate:
— **lasagne**
— **cannelloni**
— **ravioli**
— **tortellini**
— **tagliatelle**

Uno spaghetto   *Spaghetti*

5

The boot in the Med

Le Alpi

Le Alpi (the Alps) form a wide arc enclosing the whole of northern Italy. The earth's surface is divided into sections called plates. Approximately 25 million years ago, the action of the African plate pushing against the Eurasian plate caused the edge of it to be folded and twisted, forming mountains — **le Alpi**.

In the Alps, on the Italian-French frontier, lies the highest peak in Western Europe, **il Monte Bianco** (15,871 feet) which we call by its French name, Mont Blanc. On the Italian-Swiss border are two other high mountains: **il Monte Rosa** (15,200 feet) and **il Monte Cervino** (14,688 feet). In English, **il Monte Cervino** is usually called by its Swiss name, the Matterhorn.

The lower slopes of **le Alpi** are covered mostly with pine woods. In spring and early summer, the green meadows are often scattered with thousands of small Alpine flowers. One of the best known of these is **la stella alpina** (edelweiss). **Stelle alpine** even grow among the rubble from rock falls.

Il Monte Bianco

Le Dolomiti

Where **le Alpi** extend into the region of **il Trentino-Alto Adige** and part of **il Veneto** are the spectacular **Dolomiti**. The wooded foothills give way to steep-sided, rocky peaks which have been eroded into jagged pinnacles and deep gorges. **Le Dolomiti** are named after Déodat de Dolomieu (1750–1801). A French geologist, Dolomieu, carried out extensive studies on the composition of the rocks in that area. Dolomitic limestone was used to build the palaces of **Venezia**.

La Valle Padana

Millions of years ago, **il mare Adriatico** (the Adriatic Sea) covered all of northern Italy except for the mountainous areas. Silt carried down by the mountain rivers eventually formed the most fertile plain in Italy— **la Valle Padana** (the Po Valley). In the northern part of **la Valle Padana** at the foot of **le Alpi** lies a series of lakes. The largest of these is **il lago di Garda** (Lake Garda), which has such a mild climate that lemons are grown along its **riviera** (shore).

L'Italia peninsulare

Most of Italy is mountainous, and peninsular Italy is no exception. A mountain chain called **gli Appennini** (the Apennines) runs down from **le Alpi** in the northwest, curving southward to form the backbone of the peninsula. The highest peak in the range is **il Gran Sasso** (9,580 feet) in central Italy.

Small plains, dotted along the peninsula, offer good soil for agriculture. Many of the hills are used for growing typical Mediterranean agricultural products like **olive** (olives), **uva** (grapes) for eating and wine-making, and **arance** (oranges) and **limoni** (lemons).

Alberi di limone

il lago Maggiore · le Alpi · le Dolomiti · la Valle Padana · il fiume Po · il fiume Arno · il mare Adriatico · gli Appennini · il fiume Tevere · Corsica · Sardegna · il mar Tirreno · il mare Mediterraneo · Sicilia

Le isole

Various **isole** (islands) lie off the coast of the Italian peninsula. The largest of these are **la Sicilia** (Sicily) and **la Sardegna** (Sardinia).

Dominating the mountainous landscape of **la Sicilia** is **il vulcano Etna** (10,902 feet). Over the centuries, Etna's frequent eruptions have thrown out lava which has become fertile farmland for growing citrus fruit like lemons and oranges. **La Sardegna** is the second largest island in **il mare Mediterraneo** after **la Sicilia**. It is a remnant of a landmass which emerged from the sea more than 600 million years ago, before the Italian peninsula was formed.

Vesuvio (Vesuvius), the only active volcano on mainland Europe, is in Italy. Offshore, there are other active volcanoes—Stromboli, Vulcano and Lipari. The islands on which the volcanoes stand are named after the volcanoes. There are other volcanic areas along the western side of peninsular Italy, from la Toscana down to la Campania, the region around Napoli (Naples).

Parts of the country are subject to **terremoti** *(earthquakes), which may vary from slight tremors to major disasters. In 1908, an earthquake destroyed the city of Messina in* **Sicilia**. *Messina was rebuilt with low buildings in 1911. In 1980, 3,000 people were killed and 180,000 became homeless in an earthquake that struck the* **Napoli** *area.*

La costa sarda

Che tempo fa?

When an Italian wants to ask what the weather is like, s/he asks, **"Che tempo fa?"** There are many contrasts in **il tempo**. On the same day in winter, a Sicilian can sit outside enjoying gentle sunshine, while Alpine villagers wade through deep snow. In **la Valle Padana** traffic may be shrouded in thick fog.

Such contrasts are not surprising if you consider that the northernmost area, **l'Alto Adige**, is sandwiched between Switzerland and Austria, and southern **Sicilia** lies almost on the same latitude as Tunisia in Africa.

In the summer, temperatures in the north may compare with those in the south. The extreme south is very dry, and droughts are common. In Italy, temperatures are measured in **centigradi**, not Fahrenheit.

Come si dice?

Here are some expressions you may hear about the weather:

Fa caldo	It's hot
Fa freddo	It's cold
C'è il sole	It's sunny
Piove	It's raining
È nuvoloso	It's cloudy
Nevica	It's snowing
C'è il vento	It's windy
C'è la nebbia	It's foggy

■ With a partner, talk about **il tempo**.

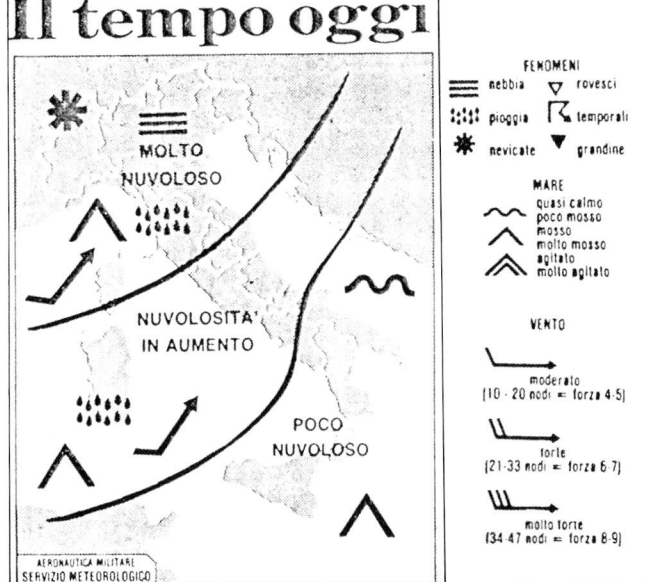

This is a weather forecast from an Italian newspaper.
■ If **molto nuvoloso** means very cloudy, what do you think **poco nuvoloso** means?
■ What will the weather be like in the Alps?
■ What do the arrowed symbols tell you?
■ It is raining in which two places?

Across the regions—the north

Italy has 20 **regioni** (regions). Some regional boundaries are natural, while other regions were separate states which existed before 1870. Each region is responsible for local administration, and some regions (**Valle d'Aosta, Trentino-Alto Adige, Friuli-Venezia-Giulia, Sicilia** and **Sardegna**) enjoy a special autonomous status because they are near national borders, or they are islands.

Una regione is subdivided into **province** (provinces), which consist of **un capoluogo di provincia** (a chief town or city) and its surrounding area which includes many **comuni** (smaller towns or villages). Every **capoluogo di provincia** is also **un comune**, and every **regione** has its own **capoluogo di regione**. There are 95 **province** and 8,091 **comuni** throughout Italy.

ORIAGO
frazione di MIRA

comune
denuclearizzato

■ What is special about this **comune**?

Northwest: **Valle d'Aosta, Piemonte**

All of the most northerly regions have areas that lie in **le Alpi**. Between **la Valle d'Aosta** (the Aosta Valley) and **Piemonte** (Piedmont) is **il parco nazionale del Gran Paradiso** (the Gran Paradiso National Park). It was founded in 1922 to help preserve rare Alpine animals like the ibex, and rare Alpine plants.

In **Piemonte**, on the banks of Italy's longest river, the Po, is **Torino** (Turin), with over 1,000,000 inhabitants, which is associated with the automobile industry. The city is home to giant car manufacturers Fiat. Two thirds of all Italian cars are produced in **Torino**—approximately 900,000 a year.

Northwest: **Liguria**

In the northwest, **la regione della Liguria** is traditionally a vacation spot. **I liguri** (people from Liguria) are reputed to be hard-working, sober and a bit reserved. Originally, they were mainly seafaring people, but many now work in tourism.

Together with **Torino** and **Milano, il capoluogo della Liguria, Genova** (Genoa) forms what is known as the Industrial Triangle which has the largest concentration of industry in Italy. These cities grew very rapidly after World War II when millions of immigrants came from the south.

Genova is the largest port in Italy, with a traffic of around 6,000 ships a year. Many of the city's older streets are built with steps down the hills to the sea. The city center's elegant buildings earned the city its nickname **la Superba**.

Il parco nazionale del Gran Parad

il museo dell'automobile

Torino

Center: **Emilia—Romagna**

Il centro di Bologna

Il porto di Genova

Before 1870, some regions were ruled by the Roman Catholic Church. One of these Papal States was **Emilia-Romagna. Gli emiliani** (people of **Emilia-Romagna**) are known as **buongustai** (gourmets). Their tradition of good eating has given the world **tortellini** (meat-filled pasta), **prosciutto crudo** (Parma or raw ham) and **parmigiano** (Parmesan cheese). Because of this tradition, **il capoluogo di regione, Bologna,** is called **la Grassa** (the fat one).

North: **Lombardia**

Milano (Milan), **il capoluogo della Lombardia** (Lombardy), has a population of 1,500,000, and is Italy's industrial, banking, insurance and fashion center. **La Fiera di Milano**, the trade fair held every April, attracts over a million visitors. In the middle of the city is **il Duomo**, a magnificent Gothic cathedral.

La regione di Lombardia is the most densely populated area in Italy. The fertile soil of **la Valle Padana** is used for large-scale wheat and rice production.

Many of the lakes of Italy's Lake District are in **Lombardia**. The largest is **il lago Maggiore**, which lies between **Piemonte** and **Lombardia**.

Il Duomo, Milano ▶

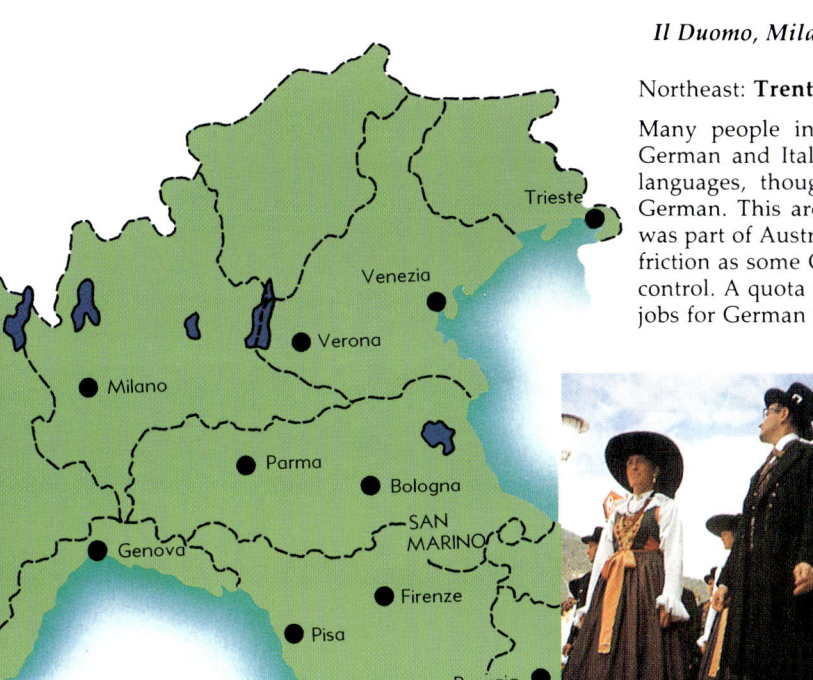

Northeast: **Trentino-Alto Adige**

Many people in **l'Alto Adige** area are bilingual in German and Italian. Road signs often appear in both languages, though many shop signs appear only in German. This area is also called the South Tyrol, and was part of Austria until 1919. Recently, there has been friction as some German speakers object to Italian state control. A quota system has been introduced to reserve jobs for German speakers.

Northeast: **Veneto, Friuli-Venezia-Giulia**

The last city before the Yugoslav border is Trieste, which only became part of Italy again in 1954. It was an independent territory in the years after World War II.

Trieste is the largest port on **il mare Adriatico**, handling a large volume of goods for Austria and Yugoslavia. The main square, **la Piazza dell'Unità**, is the largest in Italy. **I triestini** are extrovert and lively people.

Veneto includes the unique city of **Venezia** (Venice) which was built on small islands just off the mainland. It has canals instead of streets. For centuries **Venezia** was a powerful independent republic that traded with the whole of the known world. Today, it is **il capoluogo** of **la regione del Veneto** whose ancient towns of **Verona, Padova** (Padua) and **Vicenza** are home to great treasures of art and architecture.

Bolzano, Alto Adige

Center: **Toscana, Umbria**

Gli Appennini zigzag south from **la Liguria** into all the central regions. In the mountains in the north of **la Toscana** is Carrara. The world-famous white marble, used by Renaissance sculptor Michelangelo, comes from this area.

Il capoluogo di regione della Toscana is **Firenze** (Florence). The city is a showcase for countless art treasures, especially those of the Renaissance (14th–16th centuries). Michelangelo (1475–1564) and many other artists trained and worked in **Firenze.**

In the heart of the old city, **il Ponte Vecchio** (the Old Bridge) spans the River Arno. In 1966, **l'Arno** burst its banks, causing severe flooding which damaged many art treasures in the city.

Center: **Marche**

On the tip of what looks like a slight swelling on the back of the boot of Italy is **il capoluogo di regione, Ancona**, in the region of **Marche**. The harbor at Ancona was built there centuries ago because of the ideal natural setting. Although Ancona is on the Adriatic (east) coast, the harbor faces west. It is the only Italian town from which it is possible to see the sun rise and set over the sea.

Venezia ▶

Across the regions—the south

Center: Lazio

The capital of Italy is **Roma** (Rome), which lies in **la regione del Lazio**. Like their predecessors, the ancient Romans, modern Romans are called **i romani**. The dialect of the capital's three million inhabitants is **romanesco**. Traditionally, the most typical **romani** are said to be the people who live in the Trastevere district of the city, near **il fiume Tevere** (the River Tiber).

South of **Roma** are **i Colli Albani**, green, rolling hills which are the remains of ancient volcanoes.

Un mercato rionale a Roma

Il Vaticano

La Città del Vaticano (Vatican City) is an independent state within Italy. Set in the middle of **Roma**, it has its own flag, post office, newspaper and radio station, which broadcasts in 14 languages. From here, the pope directs the Roman Catholic Church with its millions of members throughout the world.

Center: Abruzzo, Molise

In **gli Appennini** east of **la regione del Lazio** is the rugged countryside of **gli Abruzzi** (the Abruzzi mountains) and **Molise**. There are many ski resorts in **gli Appennini**, including **Campo Imperatore** on the slopes of the highest Appenine peak, **il Gran Sasso**. More than 200 of the mountain peaks in the area are over 6,500 feet.

Il Gran Sasso

Roma

Island: Sardegna

In the last century, the Kingdom of Sardinia, consisting of **Piemonte, Liguria** and **Sardegna**, was governed by the Savoy family from **Torino**. Despite the historical link between **Sardegna** (Sardinia) and the two distant northern regions, **i sardi** (people from Sardinia) are really more **meridionali** in their way of life.

Along the coast the main occupation is fishing, particularly for tuna, but inland the typical image of **Sardegna** is that of the mountain shepherd with his flock of sheep. Recent luxury vacation developments along **la Costa Smeralda** on the northeast coast have brought large numbers of tourists to the island.

Many words in the local dialect end in **-u**, and include the letter **-x**, which does not exist in the Italian alphabet. Place names often end in **-s**. Some typical names are: Gennargentu, Caldreas, Nuraxi, Arbatax, Corpus de Trubutzu.

SARDEGNA

Cagliari

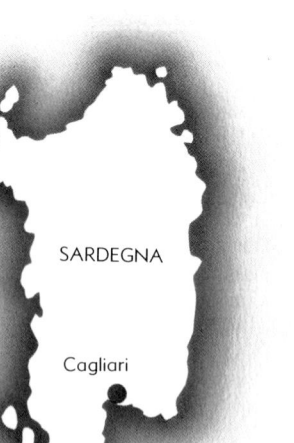

La costa siciliana

Porto Cervo, Sardegna

＊ The part of Italy south of **Roma**, including **Sicilia** and **Sardegna**, is called **il Mezzogiorno** which means the land of the midday sun.

Can you tell an Italian something about yourself and where you come from? Look at these phrases. Use them to say something about yourself and where you come from.

Mi chiamo...	My name is...
Sono americano/a.	I am American.
Sono di...	I'm from... (name of your town).
Parlo l'inglese.	I speak English.
Parlo un po' d'italiano.	I speak a little Italian.
Non parlo l'italiano.	I don't speak Italian.
Parla l'inglese?	Do you speak English?
Parli l'inglese?	Do you speak English? (More friendly).

South: Campania

Il capoluogo di regione, Napoli (Naples), with its 1,200,000 inhabitants, is regarded as the capital of the south. Traditionally, Neapolitans enjoy the Mediterranean sunshine and take life as it comes—one day at a time. Today, in spite of problems of high unemployment, overcrowding and poverty, **i napoletani** generally remain friendly and good-hearted.

In the period following World War II, millions of **meridionali** (southerners) emigrated north, especially to **Torino** and **Milano**, to find work. The different attitudes to life between the emigrants and **i settentrionali** (northerners), who take life much more seriously, sometimes cause friction, even today.

Ciao! Mi chiamo Pietro. Sono italiano e di Torino. Non parlo l'inglese. Parli l'italiano?

■ What are these two Italians saying about themselves?

Io mi chiamo Maria Santorini e sono italiana. Sono di Messina nella Sicilia. Parlo un po' d'inglese.

South: Puglia, Basilicata, Calabria

The region of **Puglia** stretches southeast into the heel of Italy. From the port of **Brindisi** you can sail to nearby Greece.

Inland is the town of Alberobello, famous for its **trulli**, circular houses with cone-shaped roofs made of limestone tiles. Sometimes, **trulli** are joined together to form larger buildings like the church of Sant'Antonio.

Since 1950, the Italian government has made efforts to relieve the poverty of the south, by building highways and railroad lines, modernizing agriculture and developing industrial areas.

Napoli

Brindisi

Reggio di Calabria

SICILIA

I trulli d'Alberobello

Island: Sicilia

The largest island in the Mediterranean, **Sicilia** (Sicily)—10,027 square miles—also forms the largest region in Italy. Over the centuries, **Sicilia** has absorbed many waves of invasion—Greeks, Carthaginians, Romans, Arabs and Normans, and the rival royal houses of Bourbon and Aragon from Spain. In more modern times, many **siciliani** have emigrated to the north or abroad because of lack of work at home.

I siciliani are warm-hearted, friendly people, but outside their region they are often associated with hot-blooded **vendette** over questions of honor, and the Mafia. The origin of the Mafia was in the Middle Ages, when stronger individuals protected the weak from tyrannical rulers. In this century, Mafia bosses emigrated to America and formed crime rackets.

History and legend

The Etruscans

1000 BC Four thousand years ago, the area we now call Italy was sparsely inhabited. Nomadic tribes lived along the banks of the rivers or hunted in the vast forests. Some time before 800 BC, a tribe called the Etruscans began to settle in what is now **Toscana, Emilia-Romagna** and **Umbria**. They built wooden houses on hilltops (for easy defense), and grew crops and raised cattle. Eventually, these hill communities joined together in a confederation of small towns—Etruria.

Flourishing agriculture made surpluses of corn, wine, meat and timber available to trade for gold, ivory, spices, furs, iron and amber. Increased commerce helped Etruscan trading centers develop into cities, including Tarquinii (present-day Tarquinia), Clusium (present-day Chiusi), Volterra, and Felsina (modern-day Bologna). There were even Etruscan colonies founded on Elba.

The Etruscan city-states were governed by kings. They were elected for life but their power was limited by the aristocratic families upon whom they depended for support. Below the noble families were two other classes—free men and peasants.

Etruscan religion was greatly influenced by the Greeks. The Greek gods, Ares, Apollo and Herakles, were worshipped. The Etruscans built wooden temples, which imitated the style of Greek stone temples. There were also Etruscan gods of sky and earth—Jupiter, Juno and Minerva. It was natural that a people who depended on good harvests for survival should look to these gods for help.

As well as being skillful farmers and traders, the Etruscans were also fierce fighters. They were well able to defend themselves against the other tribes on the Italian peninsula. As Roman power grew in about 500 BC, Etruscan power declined.

In beautifully decorated, lively scenes the frescoes (wall paintings) inside Etruscan tombs excavated at Tarquinia depict everyday life (people hunting, fishing, dancing and at banquets), as well as pictures of the gods and life after death.

Inspired by ancient Etruscan vases that had been brought to Britain, famous potter Josiah Wedgwood called his first factory Etruria. In 1769, when the factory opened, six copies of original Etruscan vases were made. On the base of the vases were inscribed the words 'The arts of Etruria are reborn.'

*Magna Graecia, meaning Greater Greece, was the Latin name for the collection of ancient Greek settlements in southern Italy and **Sicilia**. Trading settlements established throughout the eastern Mediterranean became outposts of Greek civilisation, spreading Greek ideas and influence far beyond the homeland.*

*At sites like Agrigento and Syracuse in **Sicilia** and at Paestum, near **Napoli**, (founded between 800 and 200 BC) stand some of the best-preserved Doric temples.*

Etruscan writing looks something like our own alphabet seen in a mirror. The Etruscan alphabet had 26 letters and was written from right to left. The Etruscan alphabet was later adapted by the Romans to become the alphabet which we use today.

More than 10,000 Etruscan inscriptions have been found, and some words and the sounds of the alphabet are known. Archeologists are still hoping to find a text in Etruscan and another language, such as Latin or ancient Greek, which will enable them to decipher the Etruscan language.

Romulus and Remus

According to legend, the founders of **Roma** were Romulus and Remus. They were the twin grandsons of Numitor who ruled the city of Alba Longa. Numitor's brother Amulius overthrew him. To secure his succession, Amulius ordered that Numitor's daughter be killed, and the twins be thrown into the River Tiber.

Romulus and Remus were no ordinary children; their mother, Rhea Silvia, was a princess; their father was the god Mars who gave them supernatural protection. Instead of sinking, the wooden chest with the children inside floated down river and came to rest in a mud bank, at the foot of the Palatine Hill. A she-wolf found them and looked after them, until a shepherd called Faustulus discovered them. Being childless, Faustulus and his wife Acca Larentia brought up the children (whom they called Romulus and Remus) as their own.

When they grew up, Romulus and Remus avenged the wrong done to their mother and grandfather by killing Numitor. They decided to build a city for themselves. Being

The Capitoline Wolf, an Etruscan bronze statue in the Capitoline Museum, Roma, represents the she-wolf suckling Romulus and Remus. The bronze dates from the fifth century BC.

twins, Romulus and Remus decided to allow the gods to decide who should be the city's first ruler. Romulus appeared to be the one chosen and set about marking out the boundaries of his new city on the Palatine Hill. Angry and jealous, Remus was killed in a bitter quarrel with Romulus. With Remus dead, Romulus was the unquestioned ruler of the new city, which he named after himself—**Roma**.

Gods and man

To celebrate the foundation of **Roma** (753 BC), the Romans held a festival on April 21 each year. Thanks were given to Mars, the god of war, and to the animal held sacred to him—the she-wolf.

The legend of the founding of **Roma** shows how the Romans believed that the gods took human form, and used their supernatural powers to influence the course of events. The Romans 'borrowed' their gods from many different cultures, including the Etruscan, Persian and Egyptian cultures. Each god had an area of responsibility and was called upon for help when required. The gods were represented in human form. The most important in the pantheon (all of the gods) were:

Mars was the god of agriculture and became the god of war. He was also the god of spring. Our month of March is named after him.
Janus, the god of doorways, departures and returns, beginning and creation. The name for the month of January comes from Janus.
Jupiter was first the god of light; sun, moon and heavens, wind and storm, before becoming protector of the city and state, justice, faith and honor.
Juno, the goddess of the moon and of light, and wife and sister of Jupiter. She was also the goddess of childbirth (because a baby comes into the light of the world), and of marriage. The month of June takes its name from her.
Vesta, goddess of earth and fire, and of the hearth and home.
Vulcan, god of the thunderbolt, sun, fire and warmth.
Saturn, god of agriculture, and of plenty. Saturday is named after him.
Minerva, goddess of commerce, trade and schools, workers, doctors and flute players.
Orcas, the god of death.

Fact or fiction?

Whatever historical fact is hidden in legend, settlement of the seven hills on which **Roma** was built began in the ninth century BC. The largest settlement was on the Palatine Hill, and gradually the settlement expanded over all seven hills (Capitoline, Palatine, Quirinal, Viminal, Esquiline, Coelian and Aventine). Marshy areas were drained, and a wall built round the whole city. A wooden bridge was built across the Tiber, making **Roma** a link between north and south.

Despite legend's claim of Romulus as the first king of **Roma**, historical research suggests that the first king was an Etruscan called Tarquinius Priscus who ruled from 616 BC to 575 BC. The last king was Tarquinius Superbus (Tarquin the Proud). His reign, which began in 534 BC, ended with his eventual overthrow. In 509 BC, a revolution drove Tarquinius Superbus from the city, and **Roma** became a republic.

One of the heroes of the revolt against Tarquinius Superbus was Horatius. As the Etruscan troops fought to cross the last remaining bridge into the city of Roma, Horatius held them off single-handed. When the Romans had finally destroyed the bridge behind him, Horatius jumped into the Tiber and swam to safety.

Da non perdere!

▷ Look out for monuments to Romulus, Remus, and the she-wolf all over Italy. Where have you seen one?

From republic to empire

The young republic

500 BC The republic was set up to prevent power being in the hands of one family. Two consuls were elected to serve for a year. One consul had responsibility for the army, the other for civil administration. Consuls wore a special white **toga** (robe) with a purple border.

There was also a senate, which was an advisory council of between 300 and 600 members who came from the most influential families in **Roma**. Ordinary citizens were represented by citizens' assemblies.

The young republic was surrounded by hostile tribes—Etruscans, Aequi, Samnites, Volsi. Each tribe sent its armies to challenge Roman power, but the Romans defeated them.

390 BC The Gauls crossed the Alps and invaded the Italian peninsula. In 390 BC, the Gauls defeated the Roman army and almost destroyed the city of **Roma**. After the Gauls left, it took nearly 30 years to rebuild the capital and reorganize the army.

In the Mediterranean, the Greeks were concerned about the increase of Roman power. Determined to keep his Italian territories, King Pyrrhus landed in southern Italy with 25,000 men in 280 BC.

The Romans were defeated at two great battles, but the Greeks lost over 8,000 men. A third indecisive battle weakened the Greek army still further. Pyrrhus was forced to return to Greece, leaving the Romans in control of the Italian peninsula. Pyrrhus won the battles, but he had lost the war. The phrase 'a Pyrrhic victory' came to mean one that was won at too great a cost.

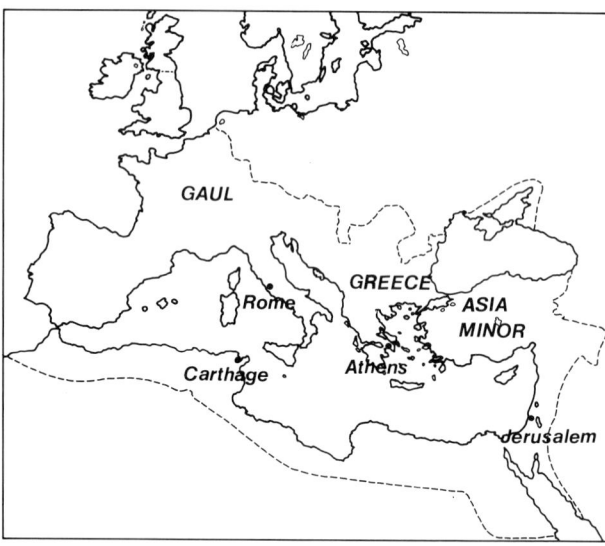

The Roman Empire during the reign of the Emperor Trajan in AD 117.

264 BC To become masters of the Mediterranean the Roman armies had to meet another challenge—the Carthaginians from North Africa.

The Carthaginians were excellent sailors. Their galleys carried goods all over the known world. Their empire was based on trade and extended across the eastern Mediterranean and Asia Minor. The capital was at Carthage.

The Punic Wars (*poeni* is the Latin word for the Phoenicians) ended finally in 146 BC when a Roman army destroyed Carthage. Carthaginian women and children were taken into slavery and the men put to death. Salt was ploughed into the lands around Carthage, so no crops would grow.

Left: Carthaginian general Hannibal (247-183 BC) spent his life fighting the Romans. He started the Second Punic War by bringing his army from Africa to Roman Spain. In the winter of 218 BC, he made the dangerous crossing over the Alps into Italy with his 35,000-strong army, and horses and elephants. On the way about 10,000 soldiers died.

Despite two victories, Hannibal did not conquer the Romans. He spent years harassing the Roman army in southern Italy, before returning to Carthage in 204 BC. Roman general Scipio Africanus defeated Hannibal at the battle of Zama in 202 BC.

Far left: The successful expansion of the Roman empire was due to its well-trained, disciplined army. The army was made up of legions of approximately 5,000 men.

Legionaries, as the professional soldiers were called, signed on for 20 years' service. Discipline was enforced by a centurion who commanded a century (a unit of 100 men). Mutinies were punished by 'decimating' the legion—executing one out of every ten men.

An extensive network of well-built roads was useful in moving troops round the Roman empire. The remains of some roads can still be seen in Italy and other parts of Europe.

■ What is the Italian for Roman road?

The language spoken by the Romans was Latin. The earliest examples of written Latin date from 6th century BC, the most famous being on a pyramid-shaped stone found in the Forum in **Roma**. *From the first century BC on, Latin inscriptions are numerous— on buildings, on tombs, and on hand-made goods.*

As the power of **Roma** *grew, Latin became an international language of government and trade. When the Roman Empire fell, Latin was still used by the Roman Catholic Church. Throughout the Middle Ages, Latin was the language of international diplomacy and education. Modern languages, such as Italian, French, Spanish and Romanian, have their roots in Latin.*

| **Lo sapevate . . . ?** |

✳ Some Latin terms are still used in everyday English:
  – etc. (**et cetera** = and the rest)
  – a.m. (**ante meridiem** = before midday)
  – p.m. (**post meridiem** = after midday)
  – AD (**anno domini** = in the year of Our Lord)

✳ Our year of 365 days is based on the Julian calendar, introduced by Julius Caesar. This calendar introduced the leap year, which occurred every four years with a year of 366 days.

Generals and emperors

Julius Caesar

One of the most famous and capable Roman generals was Julius Caesar (100-44 BC). Together with Crassus and Pompey, Caesar came to power in Rome in 60 BC. He led the Roman armies in an eight-year campaign for the conquest of Gaul (the area now covered by France and Belgium).

Success abroad did not mean peace at home. Crassus died in 53 BC and, in 50 BC, Caesar's son-in-law, Pompey, wanted to take power for himself. A five-year civil war started, ending with the victorious Julius Caesar as dictator of **Roma**.

Caesar considered proclaiming himself king, but his enemies plotted to prevent this. On March 15 (called the Ides of March in the Roman calendar) 44 BC, Caesar was assassinated by his enemies, Brutus and Cassius.

After Caesar's death civil war broke out again. A great nephew of Julius Caesar, Octavian, (64 BC-AD 14) restored order. He reorganized the government and allowed the Senate

to help him rule. He was given the Latin title *Augustus*.

Augustus Caesar (as Octavian was known) brought stability to an empire stretching west to the Atlantic in Spain, south to the Sahara in Africa, and north into Eastern Europe.

Some emperors, like Caligula (AD 12-41), are remembered for their eccentricity. Caligula proclaimed himself a god and made his horse a senator. Caligula was eventually assassinated. Others, like Claudius (10 BC-AD 54), governed the empire with skill and efficiency. In AD 43, Claudius added Britain to the Roman Empire.

Augustus Caesar

Nero

The most notorious emperor was Nero (AD 34-68) in whose reign much of Rome was destroyed by fire. Nero blamed the followers of a new religion called Christianity for the fire, and had them persecuted. He also murdered both his wives. Nero's irresponsibility and cruelty led to plots against him. When his palace guard mutinied, Nero committed suicide.

The reigns of Vespasian (AD 69-79), Trajan (AD 98-117), Hadrian (AD 117-138), Antonius Pius (AD 138-161) and Marcus Aurelius (AD 161-80) marked a golden age of Roman civilization. This is reflected in the many building projects which date from this period.

Under Diocletian (AD 245-313), who became emperor in AD 283, the empire was divided for easier government. The Eastern and Western empires each had an emperor. Diocletian ruled from his eastern capital at Byzantium (present-day Istanbul).

From paganism to Christianity

A Christian emperor

AD 300 Constantine the Great was proclaimed emperor by his troops after his father the Emperor Constantius died in AD 306. Constantine was not accepted as emperor throughout the empire, and a civil war resulted. Rival generals fought for the right to wear the imperial purple toga which was reserved for the emperor.

By AD 323, Constantine had reunited the eastern and western empires. He built a new capital—Constantinople—on the site of Byzantium, and the center of power shifted from **Roma** to Constantinople. (The eastern empire was also known as the Byzantine empire after the ancient city of Byzantium.)

Constantine died in AD 337, campaigning along the eastern frontier. Just before his death, he was baptized. He was the first Roman emperor to become a Christian.

According to legend, Constantine's army faced almost certain destruction at a civil-war battle in AD 313. Before the battle of Saxa Rubra, Constantine had a vision. In the noon-day sky, he saw a glowing cross and the Greek words En toutoi nika *(In this sign, conquer). Constantine vowed, should he win the battle, to grant tolerance to all Christians in the empire.*

The victorious emperor kept his promise. Christians were no longer regarded as outlaws. They were free to practise their religion openly.

This 15th-century fresco by Piero della Francesca shows Constantine leading his soldiers to victory under the sign of the Cross.

The Fall of Rome

AD 410 In the years following Constantine's death barbarian raids increased. The army, made up as much of barbarian mercenaries as it was of Roman soldiers, became less and less able to defend the frontiers. Various tribes—Angles, Saxons, Goths, Visigoths, Burgundians and Franks—moved south into Italy to capture whatever land they could.

In 410, a barbarian army under Alaric, a Visigoth, captured **Roma**. Forty-five years later, **Roma** was attacked by the Vandals, led by Genseric. The Roman emperor and empire continued to exist in name only. In 476, a barbarian general Odoacer deposed the emperor. This action marked the end of the Roman empire in the west. The last emperor's name was...Romulus.

The Christian era began with the birth of Jesus Christ in Palestine, which was then a Roman province. After the crucifixion of Christ in AD 31, the new faith spread to other parts of the eastern Mediterranean (some of the earliest Christian churches were in Syria), and even to Roma *itself. The early Christians were regarded with suspicion and were often subject to persecution.*

Some of the finest examples of early Christian art are the mosaics of Ravenna in central Italy. The interior of the fifth-century Tomb of the Empress Galla Placidia is decorated with mosaics which show a variety of Christian themes.

Some barbarian leaders tried to copy the way of life of the defeated Romans. Theodoric the Great, leader of the Ostrogoths, governed Italy like an emperor (493–526), building palaces, repairing public buildings, enforcing Roman law, maintaining a coinage and a postal service.

The seal of Alaric the Visigoth.

Church and state

AD 568

Christianity was to play an important part in shaping Italian history, much greater than that of the successive waves of invaders. The Catholic Church, headed by the Pope in **Roma**, enjoyed an influence which reached far beyond the walls of the city. There were Christian churches in many parts of the Roman empire, and missionaries took the gospels to all parts of the known world. When, on Theodoric's death, Italy was once more plunged into civil war, the only stability to be found was in the Church.

The army of Justinian, the emperor of the eastern empire, finally drove the barbarians out of Italy in 553, but the control of Italy by the Byzantine emperors was short-lived. In 568, the Lombards (Germanic invaders whose name comes from **longobardi**, the Italian for 'long beards') swept down from the north. They established small kingdoms in the north of the peninsula.

Rather than looking to Constantinople for protection from the Lombards, Pope Adrian I sought help from Charlemagne, the leader of the barbarian Franks. Charlemagne ruled a Christian empire that covered much of present-day Germany and France. He insisted that the tribes he defeated (Bavarians, Bretons, Danes) become Christians. In 774, Charlemagne defeated the Lombards and was proclaimed King of Lombardy.

Over the following centuries there was a continual struggle between church (represented by the papacy in Rome) and state (the secular kings and princes who ruled the small states of Europe). A succession of French and German princes held the title of Holy Roman Emperor, but they lacked the military power to bring peace to Italy. Often these rulers challenged the power of the pope rather than supporting him. But the papacy remained powerful, after all a pope could always threaten to excommunicate those who opposed him. Pope Innocent III (AD 1198–1216) said, "No king can reign unless he serves Christ's vicar".

Through years of civil war, poverty, disease and famine, St. Benedict (480-534) worked to set up a monastery at Monte Cassino. Originally, his followers were not priests, but laymen who were willing to devote their life to manual work, prayer and study. They took vows to follow a religious life, obey their superiors, never own property nor marry. From Benedict's 'little rule', the Benedictine order of both monks and nuns spread across Italy and into the lands beyond its borders.

Feudal lords

Against a background of continual unrest, the kings and rulers of Europe tried to find ways of maintaining security within their own lands. If a king could bind his followers to him personally, it might be possible to defy pope or emperor.

The Normans, who had come from Northern France and settled in **Sicilia** and southern Italy in the 10th and 11th centuries, developed a system of landholding called feudalism.

The king was regarded as the holder of all the land in his kingdom. This land was divided amongst his principal knights or followers who in turn swore to be his 'liege men'. In return for the land, they promised certain services (to fight for the king in war, or to provide him with soldiers or a proportion of the harvest). In turn, each landowner exacted similar promises from his tenants, so even the poorest of free men (called serfs) were linked by oath to their overlord and to the king himself.

On Christmas Day, AD 800, in Rome, Pope Leo III crowned Charlemagne as Holy Roman Emperor. For a time, it seemed that unity would return to Italy, but on Charlemagne's death, his empire was divided. This bust of Charlemagne shows the first Holy Roman Emperor with a cross in his crown.

A portrait of the medieval knight Guidoricco de Fogliano painted by Simone Martini in 1328. It was the first known equestrian portrait.

The Middle Ages

The rise of the city-states

Throughout the Middle Ages (1000-1450) Italian society was organized on a feudal system. To encourage trade, dukes, counts and kings gave privileges (or charters) to town, freeing the inhabitants from their feudal responsibilities. This enabled towns and cities to expand their trade.

By the middle of the 12th century, the northern Italian towns of **Firenze**, **Venezia**, **Genova**, **Milano**, **Mantova** (Mantua), Siena, Pisa and Bologna had become important trade centers. Their merchants traveled across Europe, to Asia Minor and the East. Rivalry caused the city-states to quarrel amongst themselves. By the 15th century, five city-states had become predominant—the Papal States around **Roma**, **Napoli**, **Firenze**, **Venezia**, and **Milano**.

Goods from the East—spices like pepper, ginger and cloves; medicinal products; perfumes; cloth; dyestuffs; precious stones and metals—poured into the storehouses of **Venezia**, **Firenze**, **Genova**, Siena, Bologna, **Milano** and **Napoli**. These goods were sold across Europe, often at the great European fairs, held annually in the French province of Champagne. Italian merchants also traded in all the principal Mediterranean cities, as well as in northern European cities, like Bruges and London.

Some cities gained a reputation as high-quality manufacturing centers. Milano produced the best armor in Europe, Venezia was famous for its glass.

This Venetian goblet of green glass with scrolled enamelwork dates from around 1480.

High finance

Buying and selling on a large scale required a reliable system of banking. The currencies of **Firenze**, **Venezia**, Siena, and **Genova** were based on silver and gold, so they were acceptable throughout Europe.

Italian merchants realised that buying and selling could take place without the transfer of money. They developed a system of 'letters or bills of exchange' which functioned something like modern travelers' checks.

A merchant in London, wishing to buy goods in **Genova** would make a payment in English coinage to the London agent of a Genoese firm. For this, the merchant would receive a letter or bill of exchange which he could then use to pay for goods in **Genova**. The Genoese merchant, through his London agent, would have English currency to buy goods in London. Both the English and Genoese merchants could trade without having to transfer large amounts of coin from one place to another.

Although the Roman Catholic Church disapproved of lending money for interest, Italian bankers became money lenders to many of the noble houses of Europe.

A 16th-century Florentine banking house. All transactions had to be written down. Italian merchants and bankers developed the modern system of bookkeeping, written business contracts and business letters. To make sure that such important documents were delivered safely, a regular mail service was established.

One of Europe's earliest universities was founded at Bologna in the 11th century. The first students were scholars from all over Europe. L'Università di Bologna was especially famous for law and anatomy studies.

Unlike many mediaeval universities, Bologna had a series of women professors in the early Middle Ages. The first was Bitisia Gozzadini (b. 1209) who lectured in law. Fourteenth-century law lecturer Novella d'Andrea gave her lectures in a veil, so that her students would not be distracted by her beauty.

■ Which centenary is commemorated on this stamp?

Il Rinascimento

With money from commerce noble families beautified their houses and cities. Skilled architects and stone masons produced churches like **il Duomo**, the Gothic cathedral in **Milano**, begun in 1396. They also worked on public buildings, such as **il Palazzo Vecchio** in **Firenze**. Sculptors, painters and artists were employed to work on special commissions.

Many artists were influenced by ancient art like the classical sculpture of the Romans and Greeks. Other artists like Giotto (1266–1337) and sculptors like Donatello (1386–1466) also explored new ideas.

The reawakening of interest in the arts led people to examine the world around them, particularly with scientific investigations. The rebirth of learning was called by its French name *Renaissance* rather than its Italian name **il Rinascimento**. Florentine scholar Matteo Palmieri spoke of a 'new age of hope and promise'.

Il Rinascimento spanned the 15th century (called in Italian **il quattrocento**, which means the four hundred) and the 16th century (**il cinquecento**, the five hundred). The phrase 'Renaissance man' is used to describe the great figures of the Italian Renaissance. Instead of devoting themselves to only one area of knowledge, 'Renaissance men' were talented in many fields.

La Gioconda, one of Leonardo's best-known paintings, now hangs in the Louvre in Paris.

Donatello's sculpture of Erasmo da Narni was the first large bronze equestrian statue to be made since ancient times. It stands outside the Church of **Sant'Antonio** *in* **Padova** *(Padua).*

Erasmo da Narni was Captain General of the Venetian Republic in 1438.

Leonardo da Vinci (1452–1517) is one of the best examples of a Renaissance man. Son of a Florentine lawyer, he was born in Vinci near Florence in 1452. As a young man, he was apprenticed to Verrocchio, a gifted artist who, as was the custom, ran an academy (or studio) where would-be artists learned their trade.

In 1472, Leonardo went to **Firenze** and into the patronage of Florentine ruler Lorenzo the Magnificent. Here Leonardo involved himself in architecture, hydraulics, mechanics and engineering. His detailed notebooks reflect his other interests—astronomy, cosmology, geology and human anatomy.

The Slave was originally designed by Michelangelo for the tomb of Pope Julius II.

Like Leonardo, sculptor and painter Michelangelo Buonarroti was a man of many gifts. He was born in Caprese near Florence. At 13, he was apprenticed to the workshop of the painter Ghirlandao in **Firenze**. After a year, he moved to the school at the Medici Gardens where he studied sculpture. Lorenzo the Magnificent was impressed by Michelangelo's talent and took him into his household. Michelangelo completed commissions in **Bologna**, **Firenze**, and **Roma**. Although remembered for his many magnificent paintings and sculptures, Michelangelo was also a military architect (planning the defenses of **Firenze** in the late 1520s), and a poet.

Lo sapevate . . . ?

✴ Many Italian words to do with money have come into English: cash (**cassa**), debt (**debito**), credit (**credito**). The English word bank comes from **banco** which was the bench on which money was counted.

✴ Some ideas that Leonardo suggested 'might one day be reality' include:
- **the parachute**: 'A man in a great tent of linen (sewn at the top) would be able to throw himself down from a great height without sustaining injury.'
- **pedestrian zones**: 'A city, built with high level roads to be used by people, not wagons.'
- **a submarine**: 'A device for breathing under water. Useful when doing such things as dredging a marsh. Could also be used in war.'

A nation divided

International battleground

As a collection of individual city-states and kingdoms, 16th-century Italy provided a setting in which the rivalries of the mainland European powers were played out. Rather than uniting to resist foreign occupation, the Italian states were suspicious of each other. Italian mercenaries even fought as soldiers in the invading armies.

In 1494, Charles VII of France invaded Italy. This encouraged the Spaniards and the Germans to unite against the French army. As the rival armies struggled for control, military campaign followed campaign, reducing even the richest provinces in the peninsula to famine and poverty. **Roma** was sacked in 1527 by troops in the service of Charles V, who was King of Spain and Holy Roman Emperor.

By 1530, the Spaniards controlled much of Italy. **Milano**, **Napoli**, **Sicilia**, **Sardegna** and part of **Toscana** regarded the king of Spain as their overlord. Some states—**Savoia** (Savoy), **Genova**, **Mantova**, the Papal States and **Venezia**—managed to retain their independence. The Duke of **Savoia** gained control over **Sicilia**, exchanging it for **Sardegna** in 1720. His kingdom, known as **Piemonte-Sardegna**, became the most powerful state in northern Italy.

The struggle between the Austrians, French and Spaniards continued. The Italian peninsula was devastated by warring armies and roving bands of **banditi** (outlaws). In conflicts like the Thirty Years War (1618–48) and the War of the Spanish Succession (1701–14) Italian territories changed hands many times. For example, Austria acquired **Milano** twice between 1714 and 1735, having temporarily lost possession in 1733.

Mercenary soldiers were employed by cities or landowners to defend their lands. These soldiers were known as 'free lances', because rather than fighting for their own king or country they hired themselves to any prince or city prepared to pay for them. Each group of mercenaries was controlled by a leader called **un condottiere**, who arranged **la condotta**, the contract with the city or lord hiring the mercenaries.

English soldier of fortune Sir John Hawkwood (above) fought for his own king, Edward III of England, against the French, before becoming il **condottiere** of a band of free lance soldiers in 1363. From 1375 to 1394, Hawkwood and his followers served the interests of the city-state of **Firenze**. Hawkwood was even given an Italian name—**Giovanni l'Acuto**.

Some **condottieri** became extremely powerful. Francesco Sforza became il **Duca di Milano** (the Duke of Milan) in 1450.

Sculptor Andrea del Verrocchio (1436–1488) captured the ferocity of **i condottieri** in his statue of Bartolomeo Colleoni (1400–1475). Unlike most of his fellow **condottieri**, Colleoni lived out a peaceful retirement as lord of Bergamo. The statue now stands in il **Campo dei Santi Giovanni e Paolo** in **Venezia**.

Il barocco

Giovanni Lorenzo Bernini was born in Naples in 1598. As a young child he showed tremendous promise as a carver and model maker. His astonishing gifts came to the notice of a cardinal, Maffeo Barberini, and Bernini was taken to Rome. For the rest of his life, he worked as an architect and sculptor at the Papal court.

Although he was a sculptor, Bernini was also interested in architecture. He loved to experiment. Renaissance architects had drawn heavily on the classical art of ancient Greece and Rome. As a reaction to this, the baroque style was characterized by curved and broken lines, and elaborate decorations. The word baroque comes from the Portuguese word *barrocco* meaning a pearl of irregular shape.

When baroque gained in popularity, Bernini was ready to experiment in the new, highly decorated style. The best-known example of Bernini's architecture is the colonnaded piazza in front of St. Peter's in the Vatican City.

Above right: The Fountain of the Four Rivers in the Piazza Navona, Rome, is Bernini's baroque masterpiece. Representing different continents are four rivers—the Danube (Europe), the Ganges (Asia), the Plate (America) and the Nile (Africa). Completed between 1648 and 1651 by Bernini's assistants, the fountain, with its four river gods each surrounded by creatures symbolizing its continent, was designed to look as though it were 'floating on water'.

■ *Why do you think the continents of Australia and Antarctica were not represented?*

Right: Michelangelo Amerighi Caravaggio (1573–1610) was trained as a stone mason, but he quickly gave up this career to become a painter. Caravaggio's paintings mark a break with tradition; he tried to make not only something of beauty but also to capture nature realistically. He studied the effect of light on color, and used an effect of light and shade to create dramatic atmosphere in his pictures.

Napoleon in Italy

In the spring of 1796, the French Emperor Napoleon Bonaparte invaded northern Italy with his revolutionary army. As his army moved south, Napoleon created a series of separate republics, including **la Repubblica Cisalpina**, with its capital in **Milano**, and **la Repubblica Ligure** with its capital at **Genova**. Napoleon later made Italy a kingdom and, had himself crowned King of Italy in **Milano** on May 26, 1806.

Napoleon's kingdom in Italy lasted only until 1815, when France was defeated at the Battle of Waterloo. The peninsula was divided again. **Lombardia** and **Venezia** became part of the Austrian Empire. **Piemonte-Sardegna** became an independent kingdom once more. The Kingdom of the Two Sicilies was ruled by the Spanish king. There were also the Papal States, three duchies and two small republics.

The brief French rule had, however, planted the idea of unification. Napoleon gave Italy new laws (the Napoleonic Code), removed customs barriers between the states, and improved administration. Many Italians were conscripted into Napoleon's army, and more than 50,000 died. Their deaths confirmed a developing sense of Italy as a nation.

◄ *A neoclassical statue of Napoleon by Italian sculptor Antonio Canova (1757–1822). The neoclassical style was influenced by the 18th-century rediscovery of classical statues at ancient Roman sites such as Pompeii and Herculaneum.*

Canova established himself as a skillful sculptor by the age of 19. He became so famous that, in 1802, Napoleon invited him 'to carve a likeness of the Emperor'. The statue was eventually given to the Duke of Wellington who defeated Napoleon at the battle of Waterloo.

La repubblica italiana

Il Risorgimento

The birth of modern Italy owes much to three men—a political writer and thinker, a politician and a guerrilla leader.

Giuseppe Mazzini

Political writer and philosopher Giuseppe Mazzini was born in **Genova** in 1807, the son of a professor of medicine. After 1815, when Italy was once more divided up, a number of secret societies were formed—**i Carbonari, i Guelfi, gli Adelfi** and **i Federati**. The purpose of these societies was to plot rebellion against the foreign powers occupying Italy.

Mazzini joined **i Carbonari**. When his membership was discovered, he was arrested and thrown into prison. This made Mazzini even more determined to help create a new Italy. On release from prison in 1831, he founded **La Giovine Italia** (the Young Italy movement). "Italy," he said, "must be seen as one free, independent, republican nation."

Mazzini was exiled to London after a failed revolt. His writings attracted attention among political thinkers around Europe. Mazzini's followers tried to start revolutions in **Piemonte** (1833, 1834), in the Kingdom of the Two Sicilies (1837, 1841, 1844, 1857), and the Papal States (1834, 1845), but all failed.

Camillo Cavour

In Europe, 1848 was a year of revolutions. In **Piemonte**, local politician Count Camillo Cavour (1810–1861) founded a newspaper called **Il Risorgimento** (The Resurrection). The newspaper's aim was to promote an independent and united Italy, and it gave its name to the movement for the unification of Italy—**il Risorgimento**.

Cavour was a man of action as well as an idealist. When revolution spread across Europe, he joined a group of patriots who were fighting to free **Lombardia** and **Venezia** from the Austrians. Although the attempt failed, Cavour's beliefs remained unshakable. Italy would be free!

Vittorio Emanuele II (Victor Emmanuel II), King of **Piemonte-Sardegna**, was sympathetic to Cavour's ideas. In 1852, he made Cavour prime minister of his kingdom. Enlisting the support of the French, **i piemontesi** defeated the Austrians at the battles of Magenta and Solferino in 1859.

The hopes of Mazzini and Cavour were realized through Giuseppe Garibaldi. He was the son of a fisherman and was born in Nice (then an Italian town, now part of France) in 1807. As an associate of Mazzini, Garibaldi was forced to leave Italy for his part in failed revolts. He gained experience of guerrilla warfare while fighting with patriots in South America. Returning to Italy in 1854, he settled in **Sardegna** and fought in the Piedmontese army against the Austrians.

In 1860, Garibaldi landed with a small army of a thousand volunteers in **Sicilia** which was quickly conquered. Crossing to the mainland, his victorious army marched north, capturing **Napoli**. At the same time, the army of Victor Emmanuel was advancing south to meet Garibaldi's. By 1861, almost the whole of Italy had been united. In 1866, Austria surrendered **Venezia**, and four years later the pope agreed to give up his claims to the lands around **Roma**. In July 1872, Victor Emmanuel II, King of Italy, entered Rome in triumph.

Giuseppe Garibaldi

In **la Piazza Venezia** in the center of **Roma** is a monument to **Vittorio Emanuele**. *Nicknamed il Vittoriano, it was designed by Giuseppe Sacconi and begun in 1885. The monument also houses the tomb of il Milite Ignoto (the Unknown Soldier).*

The Grand Tour

The 18th and 19th centuries saw the birth of the Grand Tour. Wealthy 'tourists', especially the English, would visit the places of major cultural interest on mainland Europe. The tour was considered a suitable way of finishing the education of the sons and daughters of Europe's elite.

The tourists were particularly drawn to Italy. They came to see the ancient Roman and Greek sites, as well as the towns and cities which had been at the heart of **il Rinascimento**, especially **Venezia** and **Firenze**. With so much to see, the tour might last several months, even two years.

Italy also attracted many artists, writers, and musicians. J.M.W. Turner (1775–1851) was inspired to paint hundreds of pictures of **Venezia**. British poets Shelley (1792–1822) and Lord Byron (1788–1824) lived in Italy for long periods. After an extended trip to Italy, Felix Mendelssohn (1809–1847) wrote his *Italian Symphony*.

Il duce

On May 23, 1915, Italy entered World War I as allies of France, Britain, Belgium and Russia. Although on the winning side, three years of war left Italy with severe economic problems. High unemployment led to civil unrest.

The failure of the government to tackle these problems brought dictator Benito Mussolini to power. He was the leader of **i Fasci di Combattimento**, an extreme right-wing political party. In 1922, his black-shirted followers marched on **Roma** and forced King **Vittorio Emanuele III** to invite Mussolini to form a government. Within four years, Mussolini had established himself as dictator of Italy.

Under Mussolini the Italian economy was revitalized. Massive building projects were undertaken; the railway system was overhauled; marshlands were drained; the armed forces were re-equipped.

All opposition to Mussolini's government was banned. The king was little more than a figurehead. Secure at home, Mussolini turned his attention to his dreams of empire. In 1935, he invaded and occupied Ethiopia, adding it to the existing Italian colonies in Africa—Somaliland and Eritrea. He also annexed Albania in 1939.

In Germany, a Fascist party had also come to power. Led by Adolf Hitler, it embarked on a policy of rearmament and expansion. When war was declared between Germany and Britain, France and their allies in 1939, Italy remained neutral at first. On June 10, 1940, Italy entered the

*Mussolini was also known as **il Duce** (the leader). Despite his undemocratic seizure of power, it seemed, at first, to many Italians that he would be able to solve Italy's economic problems.*

conflict on Germany's side. The first years of war saw Germany victorious. By 1943, the tide of war had turned. Italy was invaded by British, US and Canadian armies. In **Roma**, Mussolini was overthrown. The new government was granted an armistice and declared war on Germany. Mussolini was captured as he tried to escape into Switzerland in April 1945.

A referendum was held in June 1946 to decide on how Italy should be governed. The voters chose **una repubblica** (a republic) with **un presidente** (a president) and an elected assembly. King **Umberto II** abdicated and went into exile in Portugal.

The EEC flag

Throughout the post-war years Italy has played an important part in European development, being a founder member of the European Economic Community (EEC).

Established by the Treaty of Rome, signed by Belgium, West Germany, Italy, France, Luxemburg and the Netherlands in 1957, the EEC agreed to set up a 'common market' which would abolish all trade barriers between member countries. It would also lay down certain mutually agreed standards in industry, commerce and agriculture.

In January 1973, Denmark, Eire (the Irish Republic) and Britain were admitted as members. The nine later became 12, with the admission of Greece, Portugal and Spain.

Lo sapevate . . . ?

✳ Modern Italy's first capital was at **Torino**, which was also the capital of **Piemonte-Sardegna**. In 1865, the capital moved south to **Firenze**. **Roma** finally became the capital of Italy in 1870.

■ **Una via** (a street) or **un corso** (a main street) may be named after a famous person. What do you know about these people?

City living

Ancient and modern

Many Italian towns and cities have an old center surrounded by more modern parts. Buildings from different historical periods sit side by side.

Look at this aerial view of the center of Verona. There is:
- a first-century Roman arena, seating 25,000 spectators, that is still used for opera performances;
- to the left of the arena, the trees of the 19th-century Piazza Bra with the neoclassical town hall which has a colonnaded façade and circular back (1838), and the 17th-century **Palazzo della Gran Guardia**;
- to the right of the town hall, the 14th-century battlemented walls;
- beyond the walls, 20th-century blocks.

City-dwellers live in **appartamenti** (apartments), rather than **case** (houses). The rooms of some older apartment buildings have high, decorated ceilings. Most apartments, even in modern blocks, have floors that are tiled, or finished with marble or wood.

In old towns, the streets are often narrow and congested because of the lack of parking space. Sometimes, the courtyards of large 19th-century blocks are used as parking lots. When the courtyards are full, drivers have to move their cars to let other drivers out.

◄ *The remains of **le mura** (walls) can still be found in many towns and cities. These are relics of troubled times in Italy's past, when towns needed protection from hostile armies. Access to the town was through **le porte** (the gates). This is **la Porta Soprana** in **Genova**.*

*There are not many skyscrapers in Italy, perhaps ► because some areas are earthquake prone. One of the most famous skyscrapers is the 36-story Pirelli building in **Milano**, designed by Gio Ponti. From the top, there is a panoramic view over **Milano** towards **le Alpi**.*

Un citofono

From the street the entrance to older buildings is through **il portone** (the large gateway). If you are looking for someone at a particular address, you can ask **il portinaio** (the porter).

In modern buildings, there is more likely to be **un citofono** (an intercom system) at the entrance. **Il citofono** may have a video camera linked to TV screens in the individual flats.

*Outside city centers, you may see **case** ► popolari, government-built apartments. Huge and impersonal, the larger blocks are nicknamed **alveari** (beehives) because so many people live in flats which all look alike.*

◁ Look for **il centro storico** in towns and cities. It is the oldest and most historic part of the city.

Fare la passeggiata is a favorite ▷ way of relaxing after work or at weekends. In large cities and small towns, people can be seen strolling up and down **la via principale** (the main street), chatting and passing the time of day with any friends or acquaintances they meet.

L'appartamento tipo

Look at this plan of **un appartamento tipo** (an apartment model) in **Torino**.
- How many bedrooms are there?
- Is there a separate dining room?
- Is there more than one bathroom?

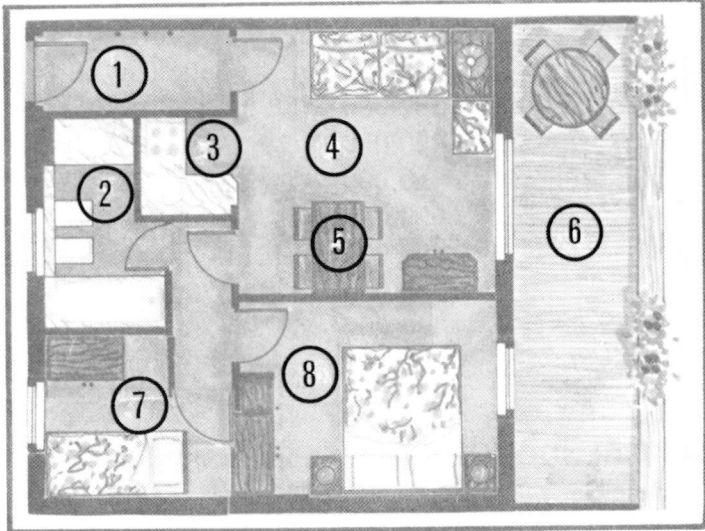

1-Ingresso 2-Servizi 3-Cucinino 4-Soggiorno 5-Tinello 6-Terrazzo 7-Camera 8-Camera

Come si dice?

Il soggiorno	The living room
Il salone	The living room (very large)
La cucina	The kitchen
Il cucinino	The kitchenette
Il tinello	The dining area (together with **il cucinino**)
La sala da pranzo	The dining room
La camera (da letto)	The bedroom
Il bagno/i servizi	The bathroom (also bathroom and toilet together)
Il gabinetto	The toilet
Il balcone/il terrazzo	The balcony
Il giardino	The garden
C'è un soggiorno.	There's a living room.
Ci sono quattro camere.	There are four bedrooms.

Some numbers...

1	**uno**	6	**sei**
2	**due**	7	**sette**
3	**tre**	8	**otto**
4	**quattro**	9	**nove**
5	**cinque**	10	**dieci**

- Which of these three newspaper advertisements could be an advertisement for the apartment model?

A VENDESI
Mirafiori via Monastir spazioso appartamento in palazzo elegante— soggiorno 2 camere tinello cucinino bagno. Tel. 868.946.

B Casa centrale salone 4 camere sala da pranzo cucina biservizi giardino garage. Tel. 539.348.

C Vendesi via Buonarroti 48 soggiorno tinello 2 camere servizi terrazzo. Tel. 227.519.

- What can you say in Italian about where you live?

Nella mia casa ci sono un soggiorno, una sala da pranzo, una cucina, un bagno e tre camere. C'è un giardino.

Nell'appartamento ci sono un salone, una cucina, due camere e doppi servizi. C'è anche un balcone.

Lo sapevate . . . ?

* Many modern **appartamenti** have **doppi servizi** (two bathrooms). Some even have three—**tripli servizi**!

In the country

Agribusiness

Nearly a quarter of all farms are between five and 100 hectares, many being around 20 hectares. These small farms occupy 48 per cent of arable land in Italy. Their produce is often sold through **una cooperativa** (a cooperative). **Cooperative** also process and market agricultural produce.

Rice, wheat and other cereals are grown in **la Valle Padana** in northern Italy, often on larger farms. Some larger farms are part of agribusinesses like Ferruzzi. In Italy, Ferruzzi is particularly involved in the production of sugar (from sugar beet), agricultural oils, and soybeans. Ferruzzi farms over a million hectares throughout the world, including Italy.

◄ *Una piccola fattoria*

*Fat **maiali** (pigs) are a common sight on smaller farms—until winter comes. Then they are killed and made into **salame** (pork sausage) and **prosciutto** (ham).*

*Citrus fruit, such as oranges and lemons, are a major source of income for southern Italy. One third of the agricultural output from **Sicilia** is citrus produce.*

*Other major exports from Italy include corn, tomatoes from **Sicilia** and Campania, and soft fruit from northern Italy.*

Da non perdere!

▷ In **la provincia di Vercelli** in **Piemonte**, and the regions of **Lombardia**, **Veneto**, and **Emilia-Romagna**, some fields look as if they have been flooded. But they are the rice-growing areas which make Italy the leading rice producer in Europe.

Italy also produces high-quality **olio di oliva** (olive oil). Olive trees have small silver-green leaves, and their trunks are often gnarled. The main olive-producing areas are in **Puglia** and Calabria.

Extra vergine (extra virgin), the best olive oil, is made by crushing ripe olives. Other grades of **olio di oliva** are extracted by heating and pressing **le olive**.

Italy rivals France as the world's largest producers of grapes and wine. Every year, Italy produces over 10 million tons of grapes. Italians often take a glass of wine with a meal. On average, they drink 24 gallons of wine a year each.

La vendemmia (the grape harvest) starts in September. Often, young people earn pocket money by helping at **la vendemmia**. Grape-pickers work hard, starting early in the morning.

This sign is for olive oil from an area usually associated with wine.
- What is the name of the area?

Come si dice?

Ho. . . anni.	I'm. . . (years old).		
Ha. . . anni.	S/he's. . . (years old).		
Quanti anni ha?	How old are you/is s/he?		
Quanti anni hai?	How old are you? (more friendly)		
mia madre	my mother		
mio padre	my father		
mia sorella	my sister		
mio fratello	my brother		
mio zio/mia zia	my uncle/aunt		
mio cugino/mia cugina	my cousin		
mio nonno/mia nonna	my grandfather/grandmother		
mio figlio/mia figlia	my son/daughter		
mio/mia nipote	my nephew or grandson/niece or granddaughter		

More numbers. . .

11	undici	21	ventuno
12	dodici	22	ventidue
13	tredici	23	ventitrè
14	quattordici	30	trenta
15	quindici	40	quaranta
16	sedici	50	cinquanta
17	diciassette	60	sessanta
18	diciotto	70	settanta
19	diciannove	80	ottanta
20	venti	90	novanta

e.g. 58 = **cinquantotto**

Abitare a Castelgrande

66 I've lived in Castelgrande all my life. It's a small village with about 2,000 people, but I wouldn't want to live anywhere else. Some younger people here are always talking about moving away and getting a job in the city—up north. Two of my brothers now live in Milan, because there was no work for them here.

I help my parents with work in the fields. We have olive and lemon trees. We also have a few **ettari** (hectares) of vines, and we sell wine to the local cooperative. We keep goats and make cheese from the milk. 99

Giovanna Campofiori

Il paese di Castelgrande

Here are photos of some of the people in my family.

Mio padre, Marcello Campofiori, ha cinquantaquattro anni.

Il mio fratello maggiore è Mario. Ha trentadue anni. Suo figlio, Marco, ha dieci mesi.

Mia madre, Maria Campofiori ha cinquantadue anni.

Ci sono anche i miei nonni. Mia nonna ha ottantanove anni e mio nonno ha novantatre anni. Io ho ventiquattro anni. Quanti anni hai?

■ Giovanna is talking about some of the older members of her family. Who are they?
■ Can you give your age in Italian?

Made in Italy

Italy's economy is based on the export of industrial goods—cars, household electrical appliances (washing machines, refrigerators), textiles, and chemicals. Approximately a third of the working population is employed by industry.

The largest concentration of industry is in the north in the industrial triangle formed by **Torino**, **Milano**, and **Genova**. At Mestre, on the mainland near **Venezia**, there are chemical and steelworks, and oil refineries.

In the south, another 'triangle' has developed between Taranto, Brindisi and Bari. In the 1960s, through **la Cassa per il Mezzogiorno**, a government development fund, a major steelworks was built at Taranto. This encouraged other industrial development locally. The Italian government also funded petrochemical plants and oil exploration in **Sicilia** and **Sardegna**. Despite such large-scale investment, unemployment in the south can be nearly twice the national average of 12 per cent.

In 1987, the growth of the Italian domestic product made Italy the fifth economic power in the world behind the USA, Japan, West Germany and France. Because Italy overtook the rival economy of the United Kingdom, the Italians called this **il sorpasso** (the overtaking).

✳ In the northern **regioni** of **Piemonte, Lombardia, Trentino-Alto Adige, Friuli-Venezia Giulia**, and **Venezia** almost 50 per cent of electrical power is generated by **l'idroelettricità**. Further south, the harnessing of water power in mountains also provides nearly half the electricity for Umbria, **Abruzzo**, and Calabria.

Produzione automatizzata nella fabbrica Fiat di Termoli

L'ingegner Camillo Olivetti

Una Fiat 4 HP

Multinational company Olivetti produces sophisticated office machinery like computers, electronic typewriters and adding machines, as well as telecommunications equipment.

*Engineer Camillo Olivetti set up a factory to manufacture typewriters in his home town of Ivrea in 1908. Company headquarters are still in Ivrea, a small town half way between **Torino** and Aosta, but Olivetti now operates through associated companies all over the world.*

In the 1970s, Olivetti also pioneered the changeover in Italy from an assembly line to smaller groups of employees working together. This was to make assembly work less monotonous.

*FIAT is an acronym for **Fabbrica Italiana di Automobili Torino**. One out of every two cars on the road in Italy is a Fiat. The first Fiat car was the 4 HP. In the initial months of production in 1899 eight were built. Today, Fiat's Termoli 3 factory in Molise is one of the most highly automated car factories in the world, producing 2,600 engines a day.*

The company owns the luxury cars Lancia and Alfa Romeo, and a 50 per cent share in Ferrari. It also produces trucks, tractors and trains.

Fiat is widely diversified, with interests in machine tools, aviation, electronics, telecommunications, and other high-tech fields. Through subsidiaries and associated companies in 50 countries, the Fiat Group employs more than 220,000 people worldwide.

I mestieri

These people below are doing a variety of **mestieri** (jobs). Imagine you are the person in the photo. Say what job you are doing.

> Che lavoro fa?

A *Una programmatrice*

B *Un cameriere*

C *Un operaio*

D *Un'impiegata*

E *Uno studente*

F *Una vigilessa*

> Sono una programmatrice.

un vigile/una vigilessa	traffic policeman/woman
un professore/una professoressa	teacher
un'impiegato/un'impiegata	officer worker
un commesso/una commessa	shop assistant
un operaio/una operaia specializzato/a	skilled factory worker
un programmatore/una programmatrice	computer programmer
uno studente/una studentessa	student

Italian style

Italy has a worldwide reputation for exciting and elegant design in cars, clothes, fashion accessories, furniture, and other industrial goods.

Benetton is a family-owned business which exports clothes to over 4,000 retail outlets around the world. It is run by the Benetton brothers and sisters from Treviso in **la regione del Veneto**.

Benetton employs fewer than 2,000 people directly. Most of its clothes are made by a network of 150 subcontractors operating mainly in the south. A sophisticated computer system gives quick feedback on what sells best. This information is relayed to the subcontractors, so color and styles can be changed rapidly to suit the demands of the market.

Most Italian companies are small or medium-sized, employing fewer than 100 workers, and are often family-owned or run. Seventy per cent of the Italian workforce is employed in companies of this kind.

La moda italiana (Italian fashion) in clothes and accessories is a major export. It ranges from haute couture designers—Gucci, Ferragamo, Armani, Missoni—to mass-produced ready–to–wear clothes. The fashion industry is centered on **Milano** and **Firenze**.

If you want to find out whether **quest'anno si porta** (everyone is wearing it this year), look in the influential fashion magazine **Vogue**. This leading fashion magazine has two Italian editions—**Uomo Vogue** (for menswear) and **Vogue Italia** (for women's fashion)—which appear monthly.

Luxury sports cars, like Maseratis ▶ and Lamborghinis, are typical products of Italian skill in engineering and design. Unlike mass-produced Fiats, Lancias and Alfa Romeos, these cars are assembled by craftsmen in small factories.

Italian designers, like Sergio Pininfarina (1893–1966) and Giorgio Giugiaro (1938–) have designed cars not only for Italian manufacturers but for car makers all over the world.

Getting around

Un giro in città

Gli autobus (buses) and **i tram** (trams) run frequently but are crowded, especially in **le ore di punta** (the rush hour) between 7–8.30 a.m.; 12.30–2.30 p.m. and 6–8.00 p.m.

Board buses through the door marked **Entrata** (often at the back) and leave by the **Uscita**. People don't line up at **la fermata** (the stop), so expect a rush when the bus or tram arrives.

As you board, stamp **il biglietto** (the ticket) in the ticket machine. If you don't, a ticket inspector can give you **una multa**, a fine of 20,000 lire or more.

Un autobus

Un tram

The same **biglietti** (tickets) are used for buses and trams. Buy **biglietti** before you get on. They are sold at **un chiosco di giornali** (a newsstand) or where you see a **Tabacchi** sign. There's a flat fare, but you pay less for a block of 10 tickets, or a multiple ticket for 10 rides.

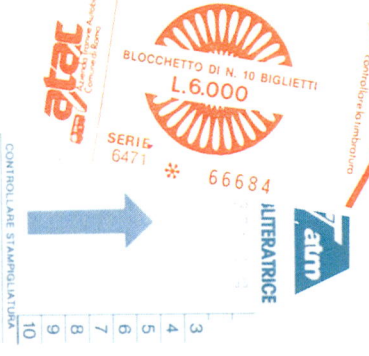

- How much did each of these tickets cost?
- Which ticket is part of a set of 10?
- How many rides have been used on the multiple ticket?

Even at **le strisce pedonali** (a pedestrian crossing), look carefully before you cross. Italians are skillful drivers, but don't always respect the rules of the road. Some motorists edge their cars forward impatiently at a red light and, if no cross traffic is coming, they zoom straight through.

Three cities—**Milano, Roma** and **Napoli**—have **una metropolitana** (a subway). There is a flat fare for each trip. In **Roma** there are two lines, **Linea A** and **Linea B**. Milano also has two: **Linea 1** and **Linea 2**. Tickets can be bought from automats at each station.

Viaggiare in treno

On Italy's state rail network, **Ferrovie dello Stato**, the different **categorie** (train services) are:

super-rapido	long-distance trains with **vetture di prima classe** (first-class cars) only. Reservations are required, and there is **un supplemento** (an extra charge) to pay.
rapido	similar to **il super-rapido**, but with some second-class seats. Reservations are not always necessary.
espresso	stops at all main line stations.
diretto	stops at most stations.
locale	stops at all stations.

You can find out from which **binario** (platform) your train leaves by looking at the departures board—**Partenze**.

- From which platform does the **Roma** train leave?

Look at these train tickets.

- Which one is a second-class ticket? What is the destination?
- What is the starting point of the ticket which is routed via Vicenza?

Even more numbers...

100	cento
200	duecento
300	trecento
400	quattrocento
500	cinquecento
600	seicento
700	settecento
800	ottocento
900	novecento
1.000	mille
2.000	duemila
3.000	tremila
100.000	centomila
1.000.000	un milione

e.g.   18.730
(diciottomilasettecentotrenta)

e.g.   145.360
(centoquarantacinquemilatrecen-tosessanta)

Note: Note how Italians use full stops not commas in numbers. For decimals, they use a comma —18,50km.

Come si dice?

Buon giorno. Vorrei un biglietto di seconda classe per Perugia.

Andata e ritorno col rapido.

Woman: I'd like a second-class ticket to Perugia.
Ticket clerk: Single or return?
Woman: Return—on the rapido.

Ecco il Suo biglietto, signora.

Quant'è?

Diciottomilasettecentotrenta lire.

Ticket clerk: Here's your ticket, madam.
Woman: How much is it?
Ticket clerk: 18,730 lire.

Lo sapevate . . . ?

✳ People living in hilly cities like **Genova** and **Napoli** also have **funicolari** (cable cars) to help them get around town.

✳ Italy's national airline is **Alitalia**. Can you figure out why the airline has this name?

At the hotel

Alberghi di tutte le categorie

There are five hotel categories:

★★★★★ cinque stelle
★★★★ quattro stelle
★★★ tre stelle
★★ due stelle
★ una stella

Un albergo di tre stelle

Pensioni are small hotels often owned by a family. They are usually in the ★ or ★★ categories.

Many hotels offer **pensione completa** (full board) or **mezza pensione** (half board). **Pensione completa** is a package which includes **la colazione** (breakfast), **il pranzo** (lunch) and **la cena** (dinner).

Come si dice?

 una camera singola

 con doccia

 una camera doppia

con bagno

 piscina

■ What kind of view does this hotel have?

This price list is for the Hotel Lago di Braies in **le Dolomiti**. The name of the lake is also given in German, because it is the German-speaking Southern Tyrol.

■ How many stars does the hotel have?
■ If the high season is during the month of August, when is the low season?
■ How much extra per day would you have to pay for a single room?
■ All the prices are given on a per day and per person basis. What else does the price include?
■ Is there a special discount for children?

Com'è la camera?

1 il letto
2 il cuscino
3 la sedia
4 l'armadio
5 la chiave
6 la lampada
7 il telefono
8 l'attaccapanni
9 la finestra
10 il riscaldamento
11 il bagno
12 la doccia
13 il bidet
14 il lavabo
15 lo specchio
16 il bicchiere
17 il sapone
18 l'asciugamano
19 la carta igienica
20 il gabinetto

– You may find **persiane** (shutters) on the windows. If it's cold, close **le persiane** before going to bed: it helps keep the heat in. In summer, shutters can be closed for shade, with the windows inside left open for ventilation.

– **I rubinetti** (taps) will be marked **C** and **F**. **C** stands for **caldo** (hot) and **F** for **freddo** (cold). Hot water is **acqua calda** and cold water, **acqua fredda**.

Just in case, you find something is missing or something doesn't work...

Fare il campeggio

This **campeggio** (campsite) is in **la regione delle Marche**. **Una piazzola** is a camping space for a tent.

■ Is the campsite near the sea?
■ If **un albero** means a tree, what do you think **alberato** means?
■ What word has the campsite owner invented to describe a place for children to play?
■ What is the most you pay for a camping space? In which season?

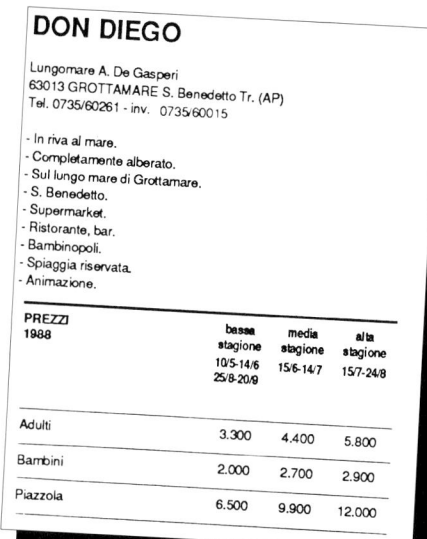

DON DIEGO

Lungomare A. De Gasperi
63013 GROTTAMARE S. Benedetto Tr. (AP)
Tel. 0735/60261 - inv. 0735/60015

- In riva al mare.
- Completamente alberato.
- Sul lungo mare di Grottamare.
- S. Benedetto.
- Supermarket.
- Ristorante, bar.
- Bambinopoli.
- Spiaggia riservata.
- Animazione.

PREZZI 1988	bassa stagione 10/5-14/6 25/8-20/9	media stagione 15/6-14/7	alta stagione 15/7-24/8
Adulti	3.300	4.400	5.800
Bambini	2.000	2.700	2.900
Piazzola	6.500	9.900	12.000

Ma non c'è il letto!

Brrr! Il riscaldamento non funziona.

Mountains in winter

Le stazioni di sci

In winter, mountain villages are covered with snow for several months. When temperatures can fall as low as −0°F, snow on the roof helps retain heat. Before the advent of snow ploughs, villages could be cut off for weeks by heavy snowfalls. Skiing was an essential way of crossing snow-covered countryside.

Italy is so full of mountains, there are **stazioni di sci** (ski resorts) almost everywhere. You can even ski on a volcano—**l'Etna**, in **Sicilia.**

◄ Hosting **i Giochi Olimpici d'Inverno** (the Winter Olympics) in 1956 put Cortina d'Ampezzo firmly on the world skiing map. Now one of Italy's most fashionable ski resorts, **il Gioiello delle Dolomiti** (the Jewel of the Dolomites) is situated at 4,015 feet in **le Dolomiti**. Cortina is in a sheltered valley, and has an average of seven hours of sunshine a day.

West across **le Alpi** is another of ▶ Italy's **stazioni di sci**—Bardonecchia. Because it's very near **Torino**, it's popular with people from **Torino** who come skiing for the weekend or just on Sundays.

There's plenty of sunshine here, too, so you can ski and tan at the same time. The slopes are busiest during school holidays, usually at Christmas (two weeks) and Easter (one week).

■ How many people can use the ski lifts per hour?

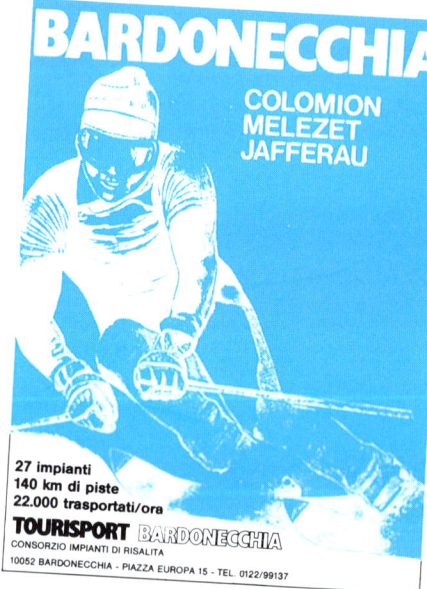

Lo sapevate . . . ?

✳ In the first half of this century, school children in **le Alpi** often had to walk a long way to school. They carried their books in small wooden cases with metal bars down one side. Whenever the route went downhill, they turned their cases into impromptu sleighs.

Tomba la bomba!

In the 1970s, the international ski world was hit by **la valanga azzurra** (the blue avalanche—blue being Italy's team color for international sports). The slalom champions were Gustav Thoeni from **l'Alto Adige** and Piero Gros from **Piemonte.**

Italy's latest skiing ace is Alberto Tomba, known as **Tomba la Bomba.** Unlike most ski racers who come from mountain areas, he is the son of a textile millionaire from Bologna. In the 1988 season at only 21, Alberto Tomba won most of the World Cup slalom and giant slalom races, as well as the two gold medals at the Calgary Winter Olympics.

Andiamo alle piste!

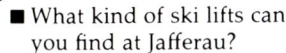

- What kind of ski lifts can you find at Jafferau?
- What time are there masses in the parish church at Bardonecchia?

Il gatto delle nevi (the snowcat) has wide caterpillar tracks to enable it to climb up steep slopes and prepare **le piste da sci** (ski runs) by flattening the snow. It can even make a seat for sunbathing.

Driving on ice- or snow-covered mountain roads is a tricky business. By law, you must either fit chains to your tires or use special studded tires.

Una settimana bianca (white week) is a vacation package for a week's skiing at a resort. The package includes hotel accommodations, meals, **le lezioni di sci** and **lo ski pass**. You'll need **lo ski pass** for access to **gli impianti** (ski lifts), including **la funivia** (cable car), **la seggiovia** (chair lift) or **lo skilift** (drag lift).

Come si dice?

You can rent ski equipment where you see this sign. Usually you have to leave **un documento**, some form of identification, until you return the equipment.

Here they also repair equipment, and have **un deposito** (a place where you can leave skis overnight).
- What else can you hire here?

You'll need this equipment if you are going skiing . . .

Attenzione!

On the slopes, you may hear someone shout:
- **Fate largo!** or **Pista!** This means "Get out of the way."
- **Attenzione!** This means "Look out."

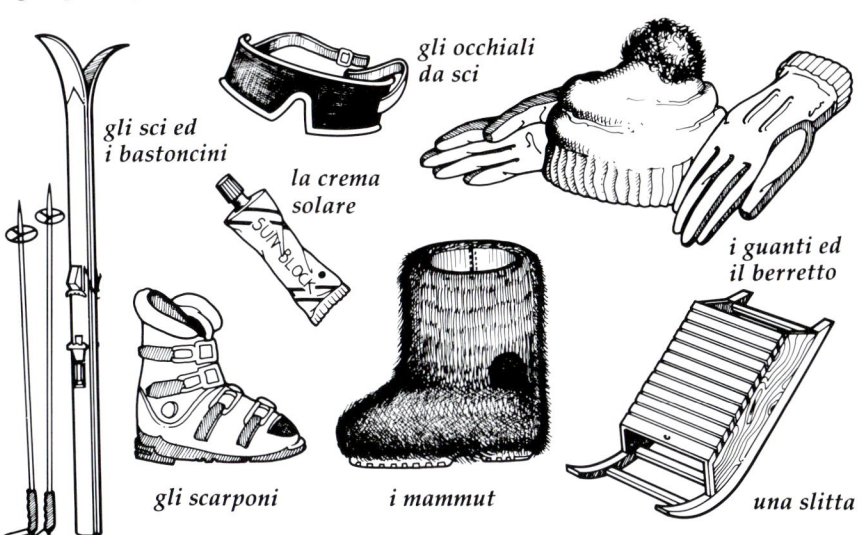

gli sci ed i bastoncini

gli occhiali da sci

la crema solare

i guanti ed il berretto

gli scarponi

i mammut

una slitta

- What kind of ski lift do you use to get to this restaurant on the slopes?
- What are the opening times?

Summer countryside

L'estate in montagna

In summer, when the snow is gone, the fields around mountain villages are planted with crops such as corn and potatoes.

*Traditionally, cattle, sheep, and goats ▶ are taken up to **l'alpeggio** (the summer mountain pasture) to feed, on the lush summer grass. The men and boys of the village take the herds to the summer pastures for several months. Nowadays, the first part of the journey is done by truck.*

■ This bin is for collecting a certain kind of waste material so it can be recycled. What do think it might be?

As an escape from the heat of summer in the city, many Italians go on mountain vacations. Even on the hottest summer day, after sunset in the mountains, the air temperature cools and there is a refreshing breeze. Winter sports resorts often offer summer vacations with opportunities for many sports including tennis, golf, and fishing.

◀ Read this resort information.
■ Which sports can you do in summer?
■ What facilities are available all year round?

Bardonecchia
Alta Val di Susa - mt. 1312

in inverno:
sci alpino da 1300 a 2800 mt., sci da fondo, sci alpinismo, pattinaggio, cinema, sale gioco, discoteche, shopping...

in estate:
escursioni, alpinismo, gite a cavallo, tennis, pesca sportiva, cinema, sale gioco, discoteche, shopping...

Italy has a great mountaineering ▶ tradition. **Le Dolomiti** offer the best areas for **l'alpinismo** (mountain climbing). You can also go on **escursioni** (walks) in one of the national parks.

This sign from **la Valle d'Aosta** tells walkers how to behave in the mountains. Because this part of Italy is just over the border from France, and because French is an official language here, the sign is in both Italian and French.

■ In Italian how would you say 'don't light fires in the woods'?
■ What must you not damage?

SE AMATE LA NATURA...
SI VOUS AIMEZ LA NATURE...

non danneggiate i fiori e gli alberi
n'abîmez pas les fleurs et les arbres

non inquinate le acque
ne souillez pas les eaux

non accendete fuochi nei boschi
n'allumez pas de feux dans les forêts

non lasciate rifiuti nei prati
ne laissez pas de déchets dans les prés

ASSESSORATO TURISMO VALLE D'AOSTA
DEPARTEMENT DU TOURISME VALLEE-D'AOSTE

I laghi

Il lago **Maggiore** is considered the most beautiful of **i laghi**. In the middle of **il lago Maggiore** are three islands—**Isola Bella**, **Isola Madre** and **Isola dei Pescatori**. Along the shores of the lake are lake resorts such as Stresa.

Vaporetti (steamers), also known as **piroscafi**, and **aliscafi** (hydrofoils) operate on all the lakes—**il lago Maggiore**, **il lago di Como**, and **il lago di Garda.**

Lo sapevate . . . ?

* Nearly 2,000 years ago, the Romans took vacations by **il lago di Como**. Like modern tourists, they were attracted by the mild climate. Many, like the writer Pliny the Younger, had villas there. There were even libraries.
* The largest lake in Italy is **il lago di Garda** (Lake Garda). Oranges and lemons, usually associated with hotter areas further south like **Sicilia**, grow along **la riviera**, Lake Garda's sheltered shoreline.

In campagna

In the past, only the rich could take vacations. Roman emperors and nobles had country houses in **i Colli Albani** near **Roma**.

In the late Middle Ages, rich Venetian merchants commissioned magnificent **ville** (country houses). These were built in landscaped settings in the **Veneto** countryside around **Padova** and **Vicenza**. Architect Andrea di Pietro, known as Palladio, (1508–1580) designed many houses in the area.

As people have moved from the country to towns, many farmhouses have been abandoned. In areas like **Toscana**, *cascine (farmhouses) have been renovated and rented as vacation accommodations.*

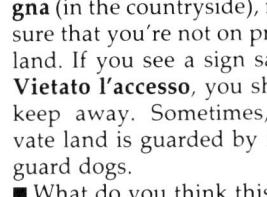

In some country areas, hunting wild birds and animals— **fagiani** (pheasants), **lepri** (hares) and **cinghiali** (wild boars)—is allowed, provided **una licenza di caccia** (hunting licence) is obtained. Over five million **licenze di caccia** are granted every year.

Unchecked shooting and netting kill millions of small migratory birds. In the area around the Straits of Messina between **Sicilia** and the mainland, 10,000 birds of prey, particularly honey buzzards, are shot annually.

Una licenza di pesca is required for fishing in rivers, streams, and lakes throughout the country. Some of the most common fish are **carpe** (carp), **tinche** (tench) and, over 2,000 feet above sea level, **trote** (trout).

If you go walking **in campagna** (in the countryside), make sure that you're not on private land. If you see a sign saying **Vietato l'accesso**, you should keep away. Sometimes, private land is guarded by fierce guard dogs.
■ What do you think this sign means?

■ This sign says hunting is not allowed. What kind of area is it?

Vacation time

Andare in vacanza

Italy is second only to the United States in the number of foreign tourists it receives—53 million in 1987. Because Italy is **una penisola**, nowhere is far from the sea. With over 4,500 miles of coastline, there is a great variety of **luoghi di villeggiatura** (seaside resorts).

Monterosso al mare
CINQUE TERRE

To the east of **Genova** on **la Riviera di Levante** (the Eastern Riviera) is the fashionable resort of Portofino. Originally a small fishing village, Portofino was discovered in the 1950s by writers, artists and the international jet set. Strict building controls ensure that there are no high-rise hotels. The town's sheltered harbor is always filled with yachts in the summer.

Because **il Golfo di La Spezia** formed a natural harbor, La Spezia was chosen as the main base for **la Marina Italiana** (the Italian navy). Heavily bombed during World War II, the harbor was later modernized. It now has the largest naval dockyard in the country—an important source of jobs locally. **Il Golfo di La Spezia** is also known as **il Golfo dei Poeti** because the beauty of the area inspired the medieval poets Dante and **Petrarca** (Petrarch), as well as 19th-century poets like Byron and Shelley to write about it.

Further along **la Riviera di Levante** are **le Cinque Terre**, five fishing villages—Monterosso, Vernazza, Corniglia, Manarola, Riomaggiore. The natural beauty of the area is relatively unspoiled, because until recently there were few roads into the area. Access was by sea or train.

The local people are descendants of pirates who roamed the Mediterranean centuries ago and settled on the coast. Despite the influx of tourists, the people live their lives very much as before in their picturesque, old villages.

In **Sardegna**, another jet-set haunt is la Costa Smeralda, especially the elegant resort of Porto Cervo. This area has recently been developed for tourism. La Costa Smeralda offers empty white-sanded beaches; clear, emerald green water, and excellent fish, especially seafood.

A little further north is l'isola di Caprera, where Garibaldi spent his last years and is buried. His house is now a museum.

◄ Display boards set up around town give information on hotel accommodations in Rimini.

Rimini is one of the most famous beach resorts in Europe. It is said everything started with six **cabine** (small huts for changing clothes) ...now its nine-mile beach has rows of **ombrelloni** (beach umbrellas) for the thousands of annual visitors. As well as hotels and holiday apartments, there is an old town with a Roman bridge and arch dating back 2,000 years.

At **Italia in miniatura** in Rimini, Italy has been reconstructed on a 19.5-acre site. It has a replica of St. Peter's in **Roma** which took eight months to build. Every year, 600,000 people come for a quick trip round this 'mini Italy'.

In summer, Rimini's discotheques and night clubs entertain about 100,000 people a night—almost two-thirds as many people as live in the town.

■ How many hotels and hotel rooms does Rimini have?

In **la regione della Calabria**, there are many coastal villages and towns in unspoilt settings. Just across from **la Sicilia** on **la Costa Viola** (so called because hills and sea become a deep violet color in the hour before sunset) is the resort of Scilla.

The huge waves which break over the rocks here gave rise to the legend of Scylla and Charybdis. These two monsters churned up the waters of **lo Stretto di Messina** (the Straits of Messina) between **Sicilia** and the mainland, making life difficult—and dangerous—for shipping.

The area is famous for **pesce spada** (swordfish). To watch for **pesce spada**, the fishermen lean out along ladders projecting from the bow of their fishing boats.

Ecco... i «numeri» della più grande spiaggia del mondo!

ABITANTI	130.000
LUNGHEZZA SPIAGGIA	15 km.
LARGHEZZA	40-200 m.
TEMPERATURA MEDIA DELL'ACQUA	27°
ALBERGHI	1.525
CAMERE	40.720
RISTORANTI E TRATTORIE	190
BAR, PUBS, CAFFE	450
PIZZERIE, TAVOLE CALDE, SNACKS	250
PASTICCERIE E GELATERIE	220
DISCOTECHE, DANCINGS, NIGHT CLUBS	
CINEMA	125
	36

e poi: CAMPI DA TENNIS, PISCINE, PISTE DI PATTINAGGIO, BOWLING, SQUASH-INN, ACQUARI, SALE BILIARDO, GALOPPATOIO, MINIGOLF, GO-KART, SCUOLE DI VELA, NUOTO E WIND SURF, SAUNE, PALESTRE E...TUTTA LA «CAPITALE DEL TURISMO»A VOSTRA DISPOSIZIONE!

Sulla strada

Most people take **le vacanze** (vacations) in August, and in the large cities, many shops and businesses also close. In **Torino**, the Fiat factories and offices close for three weeks in August. On August 15 is a religious holiday, the Feast of the Assumption, popularly known as **Ferragosto**. The vacation rush to leave the cities is sometimes called **l'esodo** (exodus) **di Ferragosto**, because up to 12 million cars may be on the road.

Autostrade (freeways) are officially referred to by numbers, but some routes also have more picturesque names. **L'Autostrada del Sole** (the Freeway of the Sun) links **Milano** with the sunny south, along the A1, A2 and A3.

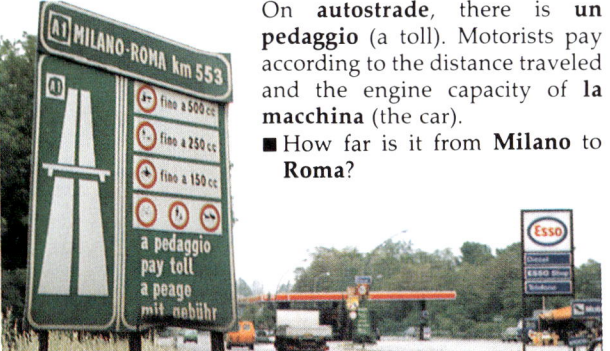

On **autostrade**, there is **un pedaggio** (a toll). Motorists pay according to the distance traveled and the engine capacity of **la macchina** (the car).

■ How far is it from **Milano** to **Roma**?

The motorway speed limit is in **chilometri all'ora** (km/h) and varies depending on car engine size. Look at this sign.

■ What are the upper speed limits on roads and on motorways?

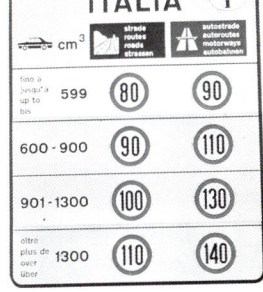

ITALIA		
cm³	strade routes roads strassen	autostrade autoroutes motorways autobahnen
fino a jusqu'à up to bis 599	80	90
600 - 900	90	110
901 - 1300	100	130
oltre plus de over über 1300	110	140

*Autostrade direction signs are white on green, and ones for **strade** are white on blue.*

L'Automobile Club d'Italia (ACI) provides a breakdown service, including minor repairs and towing. The service is free for foreign visitors. **ACI** also has offices for changing money.

If you're not a foreign visitor, you have to be **un socio** (a member) of **ACI** to use their services.

■ What facilities are offered on this sign?

Andiamo al mare!

Vacanze con la famiglia

In Italy, people often go on vacation in a family group that may include several generations—**i nonni** (grandparents), **i genitori** (parents) and **i figli** (sons and daughters).

They stay in **alberghi** or **appartamenti**. Those who stay in hotels usually take **pensione completa** so that everyone, including the family cook, can have a rest. Food is always an important factor, and Italians will often try to find out through friends whether **si mangia bene** (you eat well) at a particular hotel.

After **il pranzo** (lunch), when the sun is very hot, people stay indoors for an hour or two for a siesta. In the late afternoon they may go back to the beach, or go on **escursioni** (trips), **passeggiate** (walks), or simply sit in **un caffè** or **un giardino pubblico** (public garden).

RESIDENCE GIGLI
Tel.:071/930186-936638   Invernale: 071/936182

N. 12 Appartamenti con giardino o balcone
Comfort comuni: parcheggio - giardino in posizione molto tranquilla
Comfort dell'appartamento: angolo cottura - soggiorno - camere - bagno con doccia - balcone o giardino con vista mare.
Animali domestici: non ammessi o di piccola taglia
Le quote includono: tassa soggiorno - acqua - luce gas - pulizie iniziali e pulizie finali - spiaggia esclusa
Distanza dal mare: mt. 300

STAGIONALITÀ	Bassa 1/6-30/6 1/9-30/9	Media 1/7-31/7	Alta 1/8-31/8
15 giorni	700.000	1.200.000	/
1 mese	1.000.000	2.000.000	2.200.000

Per qualsiasi necessità i proprietari sono a vostra disposizione

Some families prefer **appartamenti**, because they feel freer to come and go as they like—eating at home or going out to a restaurant.

Look at this advertisement for **appartamenti** near Ancona.
- How many **appartamenti** are there?
- Is there space for parking?
- What is the Italian for 'corner kitchen'?
- What does each **appartamento** consist of?
- Does the price include all of the following: tourist tax, water, light, gas, cleaning on arrival and departure, private beach?
- How much does a 15-day stay in low season cost?

Lo sapevate . . . ?

* On **lo Stretto di Messina**, a mirage called **fata morgana** occurs occasionally. The reflections of cliffs on the sea are distorted in such a way that they look like fantastic castles.

Che cosa fare in vacanza?

On vacation, some people like to be lazy while others are very active. **Luoghi di villeggiatura** offer all kinds of sports activities for visitors.

You may prefer something else.

Che cosa Le piace fare in vacanza?

Mi piace fare un giro in mare.

Preferisco giocare al tennis.

Le spiaggie private

Un pedalò is a two-seater boat which you move by pedaling instead of rowing. You can sit back in **sdraio** seats and take in the scenery.

In many northern Italian **luoghi di villeggiatura**, the most central parts of **le spiagge** (beaches) have private facilities—**stabilimenti**—which you have to pay to use. Access to the sea is free. People hire **una sdraio** (deck chair), **un ombrellone** (sun shade), and **una cabina** (changing cabin) by the day or for the length of their stay—a week or a month. They are given a key to **la cabina** so they have exclusive use of it.

Every **stabilimento** chooses a different color for its neat rows of **sdraio** and **ombrelloni**, so visitors can easily recognize their **stabilimento**. There is a public **cabina** where you can change free.

On the beaches, **bagnini** (beach attendants) hire out equipment, look out for the safety of swimmers, and even offer advice on how to get the best suntan.

Ciao Bruno
Saluti da Cefalù. La Sicilia è molto bella. Sono qui con tutta la famiglia—il nonno, la mamma, il papà e mio fratello Paolo. Si mangia bene—i cocomeri sono ottimi. C'è un bel mare—tutti i giorni mi piace nuotare.
A presto
Letizia

- Who is on holiday with Letizia?
- Where is she?

If you don't like tennis, you can say:

Non mi piace il tennis.

Look at the photos below.
- Which of these activities would you like to do?
- Which would you not like to do?

...nuotare.

...mangiare il cocomero.

...il nuoto subacqueo con la maschera.

...abbronzarmi al sole.

...pescare.

Roma

La città eterna

Roma is called **la città eterna** (the eternal city) because it has been a political and religious center for over 2,000 years. On a walk through **Roma**, you can see several centuries of history. The city became Italy's capital in 1870. It now has a population of three million.

Many government offices are located in **Roma**. One out of every 12 **romani**—approximately 250,000—works for the government. The Cinecittà film studio, built in the 1930s, is Italy's 'Hollywood'. Many Italian film directors—Federico Fellini, Franco Zeffirelli, Bernardo Bertolucci—are known throughout the world. Today, the state-owned RAI TV, based in **Roma**, is the country's biggest film producer.

As well as tourists, aspiring movie stars and artists, **Roma** attracts many job-hunting Italians from the south. The city council has recently had a housing rehabilitation campaign to cope with **le borgate** (rundown working-class suburbs) and **le baracche** (shantytowns) resulting from the city's rapid expansion.

La Fontana di Trevi nello stile barocco.

*Sections of some ancient Roman roads, like **la via Appia** (the Appian way), are in use today. Completed in 312 BC, **la via Appia** led to the port of Brindisi in southern Italy.*

The saying **tutte le strade portano a Roma** (all roads lead to Rome) could describe the network of roads that kept ancient **Roma** in touch with distant provinces. *Miliaria* (milestones), placed at regular intervals, gave the distance from **Roma** measured from the *miliarium aureum* (the golden milestone) in **il Foro** (the Forum) in the center of the city.

Paved Roman roads were built with five layers. Sewer pipes were laid at the deepest level, and water pipes about three feet below the road surface. The top layer was paved with large stone blocks. Out of the total of 134,900 miles of Roman roads, 5,300 miles were paved.

Da non perdere!

▷ You'll see this sign everywhere in **Roma**—on drinking fountains, buses, trashcans, even on manhole covers. *SPQR* stands for *Senatus Populusque Romanus*, the Latin for 'the Roman Senate and the Roman people'. Since Roman times it has been used on public buildings.

As in all big cities, progress in **Roma** has altered the pattern of **la vita di quartiere** (neighborhood life). Once everyone knew everyone else. People discussed the day's events at doors and windows, and shopped in the local market. Now **Roma** is full of busy strangers, except in old quarters like Trastevere, or in **i mercati rionali** (street markets) where stallholders and customers may still know each other.

Le passioni del momento

Until about 10 years ago, fast food in **Roma** meant a quick **tramezzino** (sandwich) in a bar, or olives, fresh coconut, or roast chestnuts sold on street corners. Today it is **hamburgher** and **patatine** (French fries) from McDonald's and Big Burghy.

The arrival of fast food in **il centro storico** (historical center) has been criticized by some people. To fit in with its surroundings, the McDonald's restaurant in **Piazza di Spagna** is decorated with stone columns. Among young **italiani**, 16 per cent say they prefer **un burghy** to a traditional meal.

For a few, **la passione del momento** is being **un dark**. They dress mainly in black or grey.

A conversation overheard between two **dark**:
Boy: I've found a fantastic graveyard.
Girl: Great, let's go there tonight.

■ What does this sticker say?

Dov'è la Piazza Navona?

Some useful phrases:

Dov'è. . . ?
sempre dritto
attraversi la strada/il ponte
al semaforo
prenda la prossima/prima/seconda/ terza. . .
. . . a sinistra
. . . a destra
giri a. . .

Where is. . . ?
straight ahead
cross the street/the bridge
at the traffic lights
take the next/first/second/third street . . .
. . . on the left/to the left
. . . on the right/to the right
turn. . .

| **Lo sapevate . . . ?** |

✻ The Italian names for the seven hills on which **Roma** is built are: **il Palatino**, **il Campidoglio**, **il Quirinale**, **l'Esquilino**, **il Celio**, **l'Aventino**, and **il Viminale**.

Look at the map. Starting from **SIETE QUI**, follow the directions in this balloon. Where are you?

> *Prenda la prima a destra. Giri a sinistra. Attraversi il ponte, vada sempre dritto. Giri a sinistra e prenda la prima a destra. Lì trova. . .*

■ If you're standing in front of St. Peter's, give directions to **il viale Trastevere**.
■ What directions would you give in Italian to someone who wanted to get from **il monumento a Vittorio Emanuele II** to **il Pantheon**?

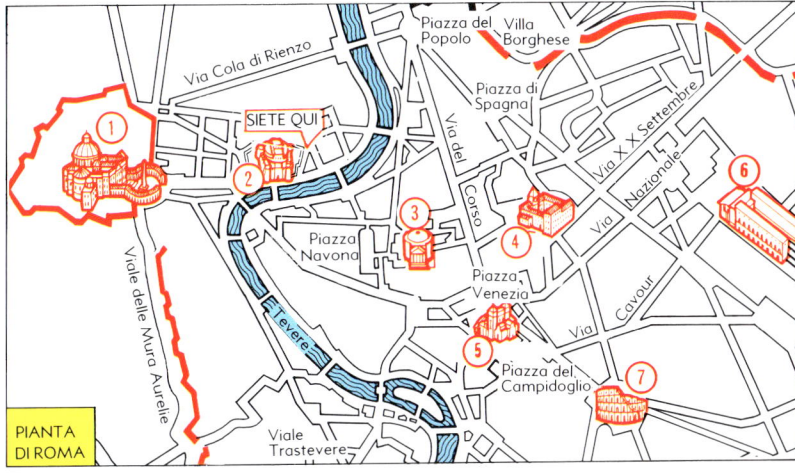

1 **San Pietro (nella Città del Vaticano)**   2 **Castel Sant'Angelo**
3 **Pantheon**   4 **Palazzo Quirinale**   5 **Monumento a Vittorio Emanuele II**   6 **Stazione Termini**   7 **Colosseo**

Visitare Roma

*Il Foro Romano (the Forum) and the nearby **Palatino** were the religious, commercial and political focal point of ancient **Roma**. A collection of temples, triumphal arches and monuments, and Christian basilicas were built around il **Foro**.*

*First excavated in the 19th century, the remains of ancient buildings in il **Foro** have suffered from the effects of pollution. The Italian government has tried unsuccessfully to limit the heavy traffic on the roads around the site. Some of the better-preserved monuments—the Arch of Septimus Severus, the Basilica of Maxentius, and the Arch of Titus—are protected from further pollution damage by green netting.*

In imperial **Roma**, games with gladiator fights and chariot races were very popular. As many as 100 chariot races a day were held in the Circus Maximus. (A circus was a round or oval arena.) There was a saying that the people of **Roma** wanted *panem et circenses* (bread and circuses).

Gladiators were criminals already sentenced to death, slaves, prisoners of war, or mercenaries. They fought each other to the death. Some successful gladiators became stars, and their names appeared on wall posters for the games.

The fate of the gladiator who fell first was decided by a gesture from the emperor—thumb down (*pollice verso*) meant death, thumb up, life.

Il Colosseo (the Colosseum) took its name from the Colossus of Nero, a huge statue which stood nearby. The amphitheater opened in AD 80 and could hold 50,000 spectators. In the 100-day celebration that followed the opening, 9,000 wild animals were killed and some 2,000 gladiators lost their lives in venationes (hunting games) and gladiator fights. Il Colosseo could even be flooded for naval battles.

In later centuries, Christians were sent to il Colosseo to be torn apart by wild animals.

Overlooking il Foro Romano is il Campidoglio (Capitoline Hill). At the top is la Piazza del Campidoglio, a splendid Renaissance square designed by Michelangelo. I palazzi at the top of the steps are now museums, housing some of the city's most famous art treasures. Il Museo Capitolino (1461) is the oldest public art gallery in the world.

In the square is a second-century statue of the emperor Marcus Aurelius, which miraculously survived the Fall of Roma.

Persecuted early Christians went underground to bury their dead, by cutting **catacombe** (catacombs) into the soft sandstone under the city. The tunnels (measuring a total of 322 miles) often started from the properties of powerful families who had become Christians. Flavia Domitilla was a relative of the Emperor Domitian who persecuted Christians. The bodies of Saint Paul and Saint Peter are believed to have been hidden for some 40 years in **le catacombe di San Sebastiano**.

■ Which catacombs can you visit on Tuesdays?

The fashionable shopping streets in **Roma**—via Frattina, via Condotti, via del Babuino—lead to **la Piazza di Spagna**. The square got its name from the Spanish Embassy which was in **il Palazzo di Spagna** (Spanish Palace) in the 17th century.

Leading up from **Piazza di Spagna** to the church of **Trinità dei monti** is the 18th-century baroque **scalinata** (the Spanish Steps). **La Fontana della Barcaccia** (at the foot of the stairs) shows a sinking boat. Architect Bernini had the idea when a boat landed on the site of the future Spanish Steps during a disastrous flood in 1598.

English poet Keats died in a house in this square, and Shelley and Byron lived nearby.

Piazza di Spagna was so popular with 18th-century English visitors that it was nicknamed **er ghetto de l'inglesi**—*romanesco dialect for 'the English ghetto'.*

La Basilica di San Pietro (St. Peter's Basilica) *in il Vaticano* (the Vatican) *was built on the site where St. Peter was buried. Architect Donato Bramante (1444–1514) was inspired by classical buildings in his design of a domed basilica. Michelangelo took over the building of the basilica in 1574.* **San Pietro** *has more than 800 pillars and 44 altars, and is the largest church building in the world.*

The colonnade and **la Piazza di San Pietro** *were designed a century later by Bernini. Along the top of the colonnade are 140 statues.* **La piazza** *can hold up to 400,000 people.*

Da non perdere!

The Vatican Museums contain many classical remains, as well as paintings and frescoes. Probably the most famous part of the museums is **la Cappella Sistina** *(Sistine Chapel) with its magnificent ceiling painted by Michelangelo.*

Completion of the nine panels on the creation of the world took from 1508 to 1512. This panel shows the creation of Adam. Later, between 1535 and 1541, Michelangelo painted The Last Judgement *on the wall behind the altar. The paintings have recently been cleaned, and the colors are now bright and clear.*

EUR *stands for* **Esposizione Universale di Roma**, *a world fair planned for 1942, but abandoned because of World War II. Some of the buildings, which were begun under Mussolini, are examples of* **lo stile fascista**, *a solid and massive architectural style.*

The circular **Palazzo dello Sport** *was built for the 1960 Olympics by Luigi Nervi. There are many government offices here, as well as residential apartment blocks.*

▷ Look under your feet when you enter medieval churches in **Roma**. You may be standing on a Cosmati floor. Magister Jacopus and his son, Cosma, were a family of great mosaic makers who give their name to a style of mosaic floors very common in **Roma**.

Venezia

La Serenissima

After the Fall of **Roma**, the people of **il Veneto** fled from the invaders to **isolotti** (small islands) off the coast. They built houses there, using wooden piles as foundations.

Venezia was ideally placed for trade in **il Mediterraneo**. By 1500, **Venezia** was one of the richest city-states in Europe, commanding an empire that stretched south to Cyprus, and Alexandria (Egypt), and north to the duchy of **Milano**. Twice a year, convoys of **navi tonde**, vast cargo ships, sailed to the Orient to bring back luxury items like silks, sugar and pepper. The defeat of arch rival **Genova** made **la repubblica di Venezia**, also known as **La Serenissima** (the Most Serene), the supreme Mediterranean superpower.

In 1508, the major European powers—France, Spain, the Papal States and various Italian city-states—joined forces against **La Serenissima**. **Venezia** survived, but, with the discovery of America and the Cape routes to the Indies, it gradually lost its monopoly on trade routes. The Turks took over most of the Venetian territories in the eastern Mediterranean. In 1797, Napoleon occupied **Venezia**, ending the 1,100-year republic.

*Most Italian cities are divided into districts called **quartieri** (quarters). However, since the 12th century, **Venezia** has been divided into six districts called **sestieri** (sixths).*

*From the 15th to the 18th centuries many great painters lived in **Venezia**. These included **Tiziano** (Titian), Giorgione, Carpaccio, Bellini, Tintoretto and Tiepolo. These artists produced paintings and frescoes to decorate the city's many churches and **palazzi**.*

***Tiziano** (1488–1576) made clever use of **chiaroscuro** (light and shade). This technique can be seen in his painting of **l'Assunta** (the Assumption) in the church of **Santa Maria Gloriosa dei Frari**.*

*Women in paintings by **Tiziano** often have auburn hair; this color hair is sometimes called 'Titian hair'.*

*In 1271, 17-year-old Venetian Marco Polo traveled with his father and uncle to the court of the Emperor of China. The fantastic stories he told on his return in 1292 made his incredulous neighbors nickname him **Marco Milioni**.*

*Years later he wrote a book called **Il Milione** which described his travels in China. As well as traveler's tales, Marco Polo also brought back Chinese porcelain and silk. Some people say that he introduced spaghetti to Italy, although there is evidence to show that pasta has been eaten in Italy since 400 BC.*

Lo sapevate . . . ?

* **Venezia** has given Italy and the world a number of special words:
- **Arsenale** (from the Arabic *dar es sinaa*) means workshop. Originally, the arsenal was the main shipyard in **Venezia**, where galleys were built for the Venetian fleet. Arsenal now means a place where weapons are stored.
- **Fondaco** (from the Arabic *funduq*) means a warehouse and marketplace for foreign merchants. There are two famous **fondachi** in **Venezia**: **il Fondaco dei Turchi**, originally used by Turkish traders, and **il Fondaco dei Tedeschi**, a 13th-century German trading center.
- **Ghetto** was the name of the island which was assigned to the Venetian Jewish community in 1515. The name later came to mean areas where Jewish people were forced to live.

Ti conosco mascherina!

Eighteenth-century **Venezia** spent its wealth on pageants, concerts and **il Carnevale** which lasted for six months of every year. When someone recognized a friend under a mask, s/he used to say, **"Ti conosco mascherina!"** The phrase is now a friendly way of expressing doubt about what someone is saying.

In recent years, **il Carnevale** has been revived. People dress up as traditional Italian comic characters like **Arlecchino** (Harlequin) and **Pantalone** (Pantaloon), as well as in fancy dress.

Venezia nel ventesimo secolo

Twentieth-century **Venezia** faces many problems. Because the wooden piles (there are 12 million of them) on which the city is built are very old, **Venezia** is sinking about 2½ inches every 10 years. A periodic combination of high tides with strong winds called **acqua alta** can cause flooding of up to six feet in the city. Industrial pollution from nearby Mestre and Maghera is damaging the facades of historic Venetian buildings, and attacking centuries-old frescoes.

A consortium of 27 Italian engineering companies has been set up to build sluice gates to protect the city from flooding. International organizations, such as the Venice in Peril Fund and UNESCO, undertake restoration work.

Venezia has become such a popular tourist destination that it attracts as many as 200,000 visitors a year, overwhelming the resident population of 80,000 **veneziani**! In fact, many young **veneziani** have to leave the city because housing is too expensive. Suggestions for reducing the strain on services include introducing **un numero chiuso** (limited quota of tourists), and **un biglietto d'ingresso** (entrance ticket to the city).

■ What suggestions can you make that might help preserve **Venezia**?

Venezia has no cars. The only traffic lights you'll see are on some of the city's 117 canals and 401 bridges.

*To get around the city, i veneziani usually walk or catch **un vaporetto** (a waterbus that stops at all stops) or **un motoscafo** (slightly more direct). If they're in a hurry, i veneziani take **una lancia** (watertaxi).*

Vaporetto line number 5 goes across the lagoon to the ▶ islands of Murano and Burano.

*Everyone and everything in **Venezia** travels by water; tradespeople and letters, rubbish and funeral processions, police and provisions.*

Lo sapevate . . . ?

✳ **Venezia** has about 400 gondolas, used mostly by tourists. Three hundred years ago there were at least 10,000 gondolas. Gondolas became 16th-century status symbols. To prevent rivalry, laws were passed in 1562 that all gondolas, except ceremonial gondolas used for state occasions, should be painted black. A family could show its colors on the mooring poles.

Una gondola has 280 different parts. Only oak, ash, walnut or pear wood are used. The shape of **la gondola** is curved to the right to counterbalance the weight of **il gondoliere** who rows with a single oar.

Visitare Venezia

Napoleon called **la Piazza San Marco** (St. Mark's Square) 'the finest drawing room in Europe', because of its elegant buildings. The pigeons strutting in the square eat 220 pounds of corn every day. The corn is distributed at 9 a.m. every morning at the expense of a local insurance company.

The design of the 11th-century **Basilica San Marco** (St. Mark's Basilica) was inspired by a Byzantine church in Constantinople. On the façade are four bronze horses which probably came originally from Ancient Greece and were looted from Constantinople by **i veneziani** in the 13th century. The interior is decorated with splendid mosaics.

Il campanile (bell tower) beside the Basilica was built in the 19th century. It is a copy of the original, 10th-century **campanile** which was once used as a lighthouse. In former centuries, people could ride on horseback up a winding ramp to the top. Now a lift takes you up for one of the best views in **Venezia**.

La repubblica had a powerful secret service, with three ▶ *interrogators. Prisoners were led over **il Ponte dei Sospiri** (the Bridge of Sighs) on their way from **il Palazzo Ducale** (the Doge's Palace) to the city dungeons.*

*Il doge was the ruler of **Venezia**. The first of the 120 **dogi** was elected in AD 696. The last **doge** saw the end of **la repubblica** in 1797.*

*In **la Piazzetta San Marco**, next to **il Palazzo Ducale**, stand two columns. On top of one of them is a statue of the city's mascot, the Lion of St. Mark. From these columns, **La Serenissima** hung the bodies of enemies of the state who had been executed during the night.*

La Piazza San Marco

◀ *Il Canal Grande* (the Grand Canal) is *la via principale di Venezia* (Venice's main street). The best way to see *il Canal Grande* is to travel along its two miles on *vaporetto* line number 1.

Lining *il Canal Grande* are 200 *palazzi* (palaces) built between the 12th and 18th centuries for the Venetian nobility. The most splendid of these is *la Ca' d'Oro* (the Golden House). When it was built in 1440, the whole façade was covered with gold.

Between 1173 and 1797, there was a ceremony symbolizing the marriage of *Venezia* to the sea. A ring was thrown into the sea from the doge's galley *il Bucintoro*. If you're lucky, you may see *il Bucintoro* passing down *il Canal Grande* in a reenactment of this ceremony. *Una regata storica* (a historic regatta) is also held every year.

◀ *Of the three bridges over **il Canal Grande**, the oldest is the 400-year-old **Ponte di Rialto** (Rialto Bridge). It was built high so a galley could pass underneath, and has two rows of shops on it. **Rialto** means **rivo alto** (high bank). As the highest point on the islands, it was probably here that the first Venetians settled. It has been the city's commercial quarter for 800 years.*

*Il Ponte dell'Accademia (Academy Bridge) is made of tarred wood. The third bridge is **il Ponte degli Scalzi** (the Bridge of the Barefoot) near the railway station.*

*This is not a photograph. It is a 200-year-old painting showing **il Bucintoro**, the doge's galley, on **il Canal Grande** (the Grand Canal) by Venetian painter Antonio Canal (1697–1768). He is better known by his nickname—Canaletto (little canal).*

The detail in Canaletto's pictures is so accurate that his paintings of 18th-century Warsaw (Poland) were used for reference when the bomb-torn city center was reconstructed after World War II.

*Near **il Ponte di Rialto** are the colorful **Erberia** (vegetable market) and **Pescheria** (fish market).*

Le isole

In **la laguna** (lagoon) which separates **Venezia** from the mainland are other islands which can be visited by **vaporetto**. Murano is famous for **la cristalleria** (glassware). This has been made in the Venice area since Roman times. Because of the danger of fire, the glass furnaces were moved from **Venezia** to Murano in the 13th century.

Up to the ninth century, Torcello was a thriving settlement with its own bishop. Now grass grows in the deserted **piazza** with its splendid 7th-century cathedral and **campanile**.

The fishing village of Burano is a lace-making center. You can see the local women sitting outside their

houses and making lace as they chat.

The island of **San Michele** (Saint Michael) is the cemetery for **Venezia**. The Russian composer, Stravinsky, is buried there.

On a strip of land separating **la**

laguna from the open sea is **il Lido**, which has been a fashionable seaside resort for over a century.

Da non perdere!

▷ Look for the carved lion's head in **il Palazzo Ducale**. 'Nella bocca del leone' ('in the lion's mouth') had a special significance in **la Serenissima**. Each morning the doge's secret police checked this 'letter box' to see if the names of traitors to **la repubblica** had been left in the lion's mouth.

Cosa ha visto a Venezia?

■ Ask someone what they saw in **Venezia**.

■ Say in Italian what you've seen.

Cosa ha visto?

Ho visto la Basilica San Marco.

Ho visto il Canal Grande.

Firenze, Siena e Pisa

Firenze

Firenze has been a center for trade since Roman times, and the chief city of **la Toscana** since 1057. It was also the birthplace of the dialect which has become the standard form of Italian.

During the Middle Ages, **Firenze** was a powerful city-state. (See pages 18–19.) In 1434, rich banker Cosimo de' Medici became head of the city-state. The Medici family ruled **Firenze** for most of the next 300 years. By the 18th century the power of the Medicis—and **Firenze**—had declined. Briefly from 1865 to 1870 **Firenze** was **la capitale** (the capital) of the new state of Italy. **La capitale** was later moved to **Roma**.

Modern **Firenze** receives a million **turisti** a year—two for every **fiorentino** (Florentine). **Articoli di pelle** (luxury leather goods) are produced in **Firenze** as they have been for centuries.

Lorenzo de' Medici (1449–92), known as il Magnifico (the Magnificent), was Cosimo's grandson. Il Magnifico was a brilliant statesman and a patron of the arts. He sponsored artists, musicians, poets, architects and philosophers.

Many works of art commissioned by il Magnifico can be seen in the museums of the city. In this painting, Primavera (Spring) by Sandro Botticelli (1445–1510), il Magnifico appears on the left as the god Mercury. The picture now hangs in la Galleria degli Uffizi (the Uffizi Gallery).

Lo sapevate . . . ?

✳ Pinocchio, the puppet whose nose grew and grew because he told lies, was 'born' in **Toscana**. Carlo Lorenzini, pen name Carlo Collodi, wrote *Le Avventure di Pinocchio* in 1883. At Collodi, where he lived, there is now **il parco di Pinocchio**, where you can see sculptures of characters from the book.

Vuole un gelato?

Italy is famous for its **gelati** (ice creams). Some **gusti** (flavors) to try:

pistacchio	pistachio
fragola	strawberry
nocciola	hazelnut
cocco	coconut
limone	lemon
caffè	coffee
cioccolato	chocolate

Ask for your ice cream **con panna** and you can have whipped cream on it.

■ Ask someone if they want an ice cream.

Vuole un gelato?

■ Say what flavor you want.

Sì, grazie, un gelato al cioccolato.

Sì, grazie, un gelato alla fragola con panna.

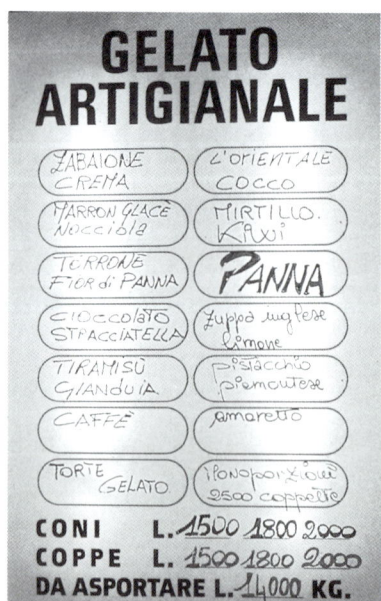

Look at this list of ice creams.
■ How much do cones cost?
■ How do you say 'take out' in Italian?

Siena

According to legend Siena was founded by the sons of Remus, so it's not surprising that the city's emblem is a she-wolf. Like **Venezia**, **Firenze** and Pisa, Siena became an independent **repubblica** as it grew rich from banking and the wool trade during the Middle Ages.

Siena resisted several attempts by its trading rival **Firenze** to capture the city. In 1230, **i fiorentini** even resorted to catapulting dead donkeys over the walls of Siena to try and start an epidemic. Although **i senesi** defeated **i fiorentini** at the Battle of Montaperti in 1260, Siena finally became a dependency of **Firenze**.

At the height of Siena's splendor between 1287 and 1355, **il Palazzo Pubblico** (the Town Hall), **il Duomo** (the Cathedral), and many private palaces were built on or near **la Piazza del Campo**.

✳ **Palio** comes from **pallium**, the Latin for a piece of cloth. At first, the prize was cloth, now it is a banner of the Virgin.

Pisa

In the 11th century, **Pisa** was an important seaport and the center of an independent republic which controlled the islands of Corsica and **Sardegna**, and the Balearic Islands off the coast of Spain. When **i genovese** destroyed the Pisan navy in 1284, the Pisan Republic's power began to decline. Around the same time, silt from the river Arno finally blocked off Pisa's access to the sea. The city now stands seven miles from the sea.

Le statistiche della Torre Pendente
Altezza lato nord: 52.22 metri
Altezza lato sud: 55.52 metri
Pendenza: 4.50 metri

It is said that physicist and astronomer Galileo Galilei proved that objects of different masses fall at the same speed, by dropping weights from the top of **la Torre Pendente** (the Leaning Tower).

La Torre Pendente is **il campanile** of Pisa Cathedral. Work began on the tower in 1173, but it started to lean before it was finished, because it was built on sand. No one has been able to suggest how to stop **la Torre Pendente** leaning. If it continues to lean at the same rate, in 200 years it will fall down.

*While a teacher at **l'Università di Padova** (Padua University), Galileo Galilei (1564-1642) developed a telescope to study the sky. He realized that the sun—and not the earth—was the center of the solar system. The Roman Catholic Church became suspicious of Galileo's theories, claiming that they were contrary to its teachings. In 1633, Galileo was forced to declare publicly that the earth did not move and was therefore at the center of the universe. Afterward, he is said to have muttered under his breath **"Eppur si muove"** ("But it does move").*

Twice a year in July and August, 10 bareback riders in medieval costume take part in **il Palio**, a dramatic race round Siena's fan-shaped **Piazza del Campo**. Each rider wears the colors of **una contrada**, the city district that he represents. There are 17 **contrade**, but only 10 of them, (chosen by lot) take part in **il Palio**.

Most of **le contrade** are named after animals or birds, like **l'oca** (goose) or **l'istrice** (hedgehog). The heraldic emblems of **le contrade** are embroidered on flags which are tossed in the air before the race. The winning **contrada** receives **il palio**, the banner from which the race gets its name. Afterward, the winning rider—and horse—attend a victory banquet.

*Santa Caterina (St. Catherine of Siena) is Italy's patron saint. Caterina Benincasa (1347–1380) was the 24th of 25 children of a Sienese cloth dyer. From early childhood, **Caterina** had holy visions. At the age of 16 she became a nun, nursing the sick. She lived on sips of water and communion wafers and slept for only one hour out of 48.*

*This frail girl sent letters with advice for kings and popes. In 1376, she visited Pope Gregory XI at Avignon in France. Her visit helped persuade him to return to **Roma**. The popes had been absent from **Roma** for almost 70 years.*

Lo sapevate . . . ?

✱ *San Francesco (St. Francis of Assisi) is also patron saint of Italy. He was born in 1182, the son of a cloth merchant from Assisi in Umbria.*

*In 1205, he gave away all he had, and went to preach around Italy. **Il Poverello**, (from **povero**, meaning poor), as he is also known, later founded a religious order—the Franciscans.*

Visitare Firenze, Siena e Pisa

Firenze

The giant dome of **il Duomo** (the cathedral) dominates the skyline of **Firenze**. The dome took nearly 16 years to complete. When finished in 1436, it was the largest and highest (348 ft high) of its time. No supporting scaffolding was used. Goldsmith-turned-architect Filippo Brunelleschi designed the dome to be built up in a series of rings.

The interior of the dome is painted with a fresco of *The Last Judgement*. There are stained glass windows based on drawings by Donatello, Lorenzo Ghiberti, Paolo Uccello and Andrea del Castagno.

Da non perdere!

▷ Look for the portrait of himself that Ghiberti put on **la Porta del Paradiso**.

▷ **La Piazza della Signoria** is like an open-air sculpture museum. It has several statues by artists like Donatello and Michelangelo.

◁ Near **il Mercato Nuovo** is **il Porcellino**, a 16th-century bronze boar. His nose is shiny, because generations of **fiorentini** have touched his nose for luck as they go by.

*The 14th-century **Ponte Vecchio** (the Old Bridge) is lined with ▶ jewelers' shops. Cosimo I, used the bridge to go from **gli Uffizi** (the government offices) to **il Palazzo Pitti**. He found it disagreeable to walk past butchers' shops on the bridge, and ordered that jewelers' shops to be put there instead. Nowadays, after the shops close, people come to hear street musicians play.*

The three entrance doors of the 11th-century **Battistero** are world famous. The southern entrance doors were designed by Pisan sculptor Andrea Pisano (1290–1348) and show the life of John the Baptist.

Florentine goldsmith Lorenzo Ghiberti (1378–1455) spent more than 20 years working on the bronze relief scenes from the New Testament for the north doors. His sculptures of Old Testament themes for the east doors took him 27 years. Michelangelo said that the east doors of **il Battistero** were worthy of being **la Porta del Paradiso** (the Gates of Paradise).

La Porta del Paradiso

Il **Palazzo Pitti** (1458) is typical of the solid style of Renaissance palaces built in **Firenze**. It now has a large collection of paintings by **Raffaello** (Raphael) and **Tiziano**.

Behind il **Palazzo Pitti** is **il Giardino di Boboli**, a 16th-century terraced garden with ancient and Renaissance sculptures.

Gli Uffizi was a Renaissance palace which contained **gli uffizi** (offices) for the Medici administration. Now it is a gallery which has works by Botticelli, Tintoretto, Giotto, **Raffaello** and Leonardo da Vinci. Many of the paintings were commissioned by the Medici family. **Il Palazzo del Bargello** is another medieval palace which now houses a collection of sculpture that includes works by Michelangelo and Donatello.

Siena e Pisa

*Siena is one of Italy's best-preserved medieval towns. At ▶ the center of the town is **la Piazza del Campo**, the main square. On **la piazza** is the battlemented **Palazzo Pubblico** (the town hall) which was built between 1288 and 1320. The building is still used as a town hall, just as it was six and a half centuries ago.*

*Next to **il Palazzo Pubblico** is the 286½ feet-high* **campanile** *(bell tower) called **la Torre del Mangia**. It was built between 1338 and 1348, and is called after its first bellringer, Mangia. From the top of the tower there is a panoramic view of Siena and the surrounding country-side.*

*A short walk away is **il Duomo**, built between the 12th and 14th centuries. Different color marble was used to decorate both the interior and the façade of the cathedral.*

Da non perdere!

▷ In Siena, take a walk along narrow medieval streets, like **la Via di Città** or **la Via Banchi di Sopra**. Look for the **contrade** signs hanging on the walls.

Many medieval **palazzi** and churches can also be visited—il **palazzo Chigi-Saracini**, il **palazzo Piccolomini** or il **Battistero di San Giovanni**.

*La Piazza del Duomo contains the best-known monu- ▶ ments in Pisa. The Romanesque **Duomo** was built be- tween 1068 and 1118. The exterior is decorated with bands of marble. Inside is a pulpit that was carved by Pisan sculptor Giovanni Pisano. Opposite it hangs the bronze lamp which is said to have inspired Galileo's theory on the movement of pendulums.*

*Next to **il Duomo** is its bell tower, **la Torre Pendente** (the Leaning Tower). It was built by another member of the Pisano family, Bonanno Pisano. If you climb up the 294 steps, you will have a feeling of being pulled to one side.*

*The circular **Battistero** was built over a period of 250 years and was completed in 1400. The pulpit is by Nicolò Pisano, father of Giovanni.*

*To the north of **il Duomo** is **il Campo Santo**. This 13th-century cemetery contains 600 tombstones and several frescoes.*

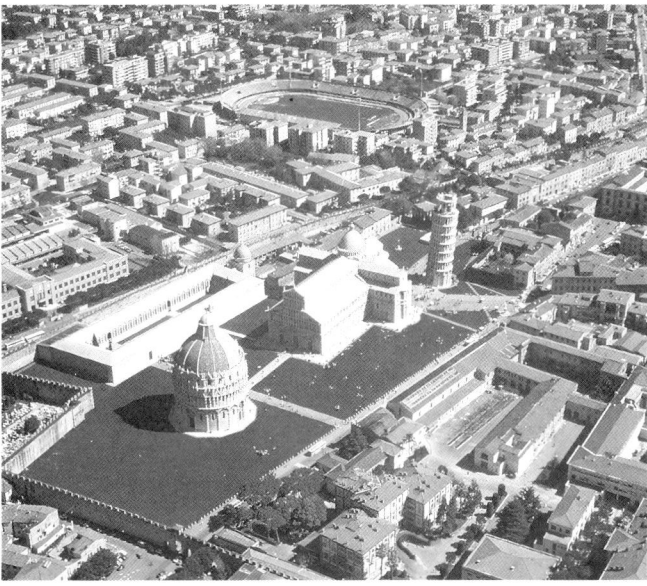

Napoli ed il Golfo di Napoli

Napoli

Napoli (Naples) was founded by the Greeks in about 600 BC. They called it *Neapolis* meaning new city. In the 4th century AD, **Napoli** was conquered by the Romans. Among the first tourists to enjoy the area's mild winters were Emperors Tiberius and Nero. From the 11th to the 19th century, **Napoli** was ruled by the French, Spanish, Austrians and French again, before Giuseppe Garibaldi made it part of united Italy in 1860.

Modern **Napoli**, with a population of 1,206,000, is the third largest Italian city. Its port is the busiest passenger port and the second busiest trading port in Italy.

Because of its position between hills and sea, **Napoli** has not been able to expand like other large Italian cities. The narrow streets are noisy and congested with traffic. Overcrowding has meant that slum areas have grown up in the city, although work is now underway to clear these.

*Looking down a narrow street in il **quartiere di Spacca-Napoli** (the Spacca-Napoli area), the oldest part of the city.*

*People from **Napoli** are called i **napoletani**. In English, they are called Neapolitans, after the original Greek name for their city. **I napoletani** are known for the way they 'talk' with their hands, and for their love of music. Popular songs like **O Sole Mio**, **Funiculi-Funiculà**, and **Santa Lucia**, all originated in **Napoli**.*

Lo sapevate . . . ?

* American gangster Al Capone (1899–1947), who dominated organized crime in 1920s Chicago, was born in **Napoli**.
* **Pomodori** (tomatoes) are an important ingredient in Italian cooking. They are especially associated with the south, but they do not originate there. Tomatoes were introduced from the Americas in the 17th century. Before that, pizza was flat bread seasoned only with olive oil and garlic.

Che ora è?

If you need to ask the time in Italian, remember that one o' clock is singular—**l'una**, while other times are plural—**le tre**.

It's one o' clock.	**È l'una.**
It's two o' clock.	**Sono le due.**
It's a quarter after five.	**Sono le cinque e un quarto.**
It's a quarter of ten.	**Sono le dieci meno un quarto.**
It's one thirty.	**È l'una e mezzo.**

Sono le sette e ventuno.

■ Say in Italian what the time on this clock is?

Il Golfo di Napoli

Tourism is not a modern phenomenon around **il Golfo di Napoli** (the Bay of Naples). Many of the towns and islands around **il Golfo** have been resorts since Roman times. The Emperor Tiberius retired to **Capri** (the Island of Goats). At his palace, the Villa Jovi, you can still see the cliff over which unwelcome visitors were thrown.

On the mainland, steep limestone cliffs plunge into the sea. Clinging to the hillside is the town of Sorrento, a place of relaxation for visitors for more than 2,500 years.

To the west of **Napoli** are **i Campi Flegrei** (Phlegrean—or burning—Fields). This is a volcanic area with hot springs, jets of steam and sulphurous gases that rise from the ground or from the sea. Several lakes have formed in the craters of extinct volcanoes. **Il lago d'Averno** (Lake Avernus) was thought by the Greeks and Romans to be the entrance to the Underworld, where people went when they died.

Sorrento ▶

Il Vesuvio

*Vesuvio dominates the landscape around **il Golfo**. Its most famous eruption was in AD 79, when the towns of Pompeii and Herculaneum were destroyed. Before that, few people realized **Vesuvio** was a volcano. Trees grew up to the summit, and the lower slopes were intensively farmed.*

*On 24th August, AD 79, a violent eruption blew away the top of **Vesuvio**. The Roman writer Pliny the Younger saw a huge cloud, shaped like a pine tree with spreading branches at the top, which rose into the sky and blocked out the midday sun.*

*Pliny's uncle, the Elder Pliny, was admiral of the Roman fleet based at Misenum to the west of **Napoli**. To help evacuate the towns at the foot of **Vesuvio** and also out of scientific curiosity, he set sail into a storm of ash and red-hot stones. Two days later, his body was recovered. He had suffocated from poisonous gases. By that time, both Pompeii and Herculaneum had been destroyed, many of their inhabitants killed, and a new cone had appeared in the old crater of the volcano.*

This map of **il Golfo di Napoli** is from a shop which sells jewelry and ornaments made of **corallo** (coral).

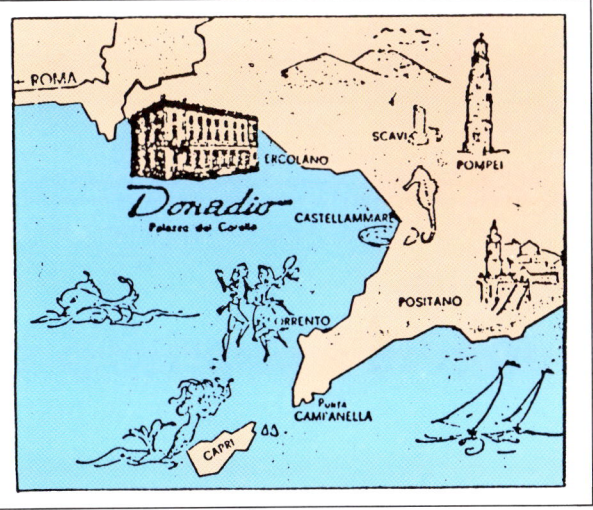

■ What are the modern Italian names for Herculaneum and Pompeii?

Da non perdere!

▷ **Mozzarella** is the cheese used on pizzas. The best **mozzarella** is made from buffalo milk, and it originates in **la regione della Campania**. Most of Italy's buffaloes are found in this area.

Visitare il Golfo di Napoli

The best way to arrive in **Napoli** is by sea. Across the bay is a view of the volcano **Vesuvio**. The harbor entrance is guarded by **il Castel Nuovo**, although this 'new castle' is 700 years old. Nearby are **il Teatro San Carlo** and **il Palazzo Reale** (the Royal Palace).

The patron saint of **Napoli** is **San Gennaro**. In **il Duomo di San Gennaro** (the Cathedral of St. Januarius) are two vials of the saint's congealed blood. Twice a year, on the first Saturday in May and on 19th September, the blood miraculously liquifies. If this does not happen, it is said that disaster will strike **Napoli**.

*Il Castel Nuovo is also called **il Maschio Angioino** (the Angevin Castle), because it is modeled on a castle in Angers (France). Charles of Anjou came from France and conquered **Napoli** and **Sicilia** in 1246. The castle was built in 1282 by French architect Pierre d'Agincourt.*

*Housed in a 16th-century **palazzo** is a treasure trove of Greek and Roman antiquities, many of which belonged to the aristocratic Farnese family. In **il Museo Archeologico Nazionale** are some of the most interesting finds excavated at Pompeii and Herculaneum. These include mosaics, frescoes and sculptures.*

This mosaic found at Pompeii shows a fierce guard dog. Cave canem is Latin for 'beware of the dog'. Look on page 37 for the modern Italian equivalent.

*Take a stroll through **la Galleria Umberto** near **la Piazza del Plebiscito**. **La Galleria** has four arcades of shops and cafés.*

Sorrento e Capri

Sorrento is the terminus for **la Circumvesuviana**, the railway which runs from **Napoli** to Herculaneum, Pompeii, and Sorrento. The road to Sorrento twists and turns along the cliff tops. Beyond Sorrento, the road continues to Positano and Amalfi. Along the 18-mile stretch of road to Amalfi there are over 750 major bends.

◀ *From **Napoli** and from Sorrento you can cross to Capri by **aliscafo** (hydrofoil) or by **traghetto** (ferry).*

Da non perdere!

NA P92866

▷ Car number plates show the province where the car is registered, e.g., **NA** is for **Napoli**.

■ How long does it take to go to **Napoli**?

*The island of Capri suffers from overcrowding during its short tourist season. Steep limestone cliffs are scenic but leave little room for beaches. **Una funicolare** (cable car) links Marina Grande, where most tourists land, to the town of Capri.*

*The main attraction is **la Grotta Azzurra** (the Blue Grotto). If the sun is shining and the sea is calm, the refraction of the light through the water makes it seem a fluorescent blue.*

Ercolano e Pompei

Herculaneum's modern Italian name is **Ercolano**. In AD 79, it had a population of approximately 5,000. It was a fishing port and a resort town. The streets were laid out on a typical Roman grid pattern. In the center of the town were a sports ground (*palestra*), the forum, public baths and a theater. The villas of the richer inhabitants were on the outskirts of Herculaneum.

When **Vesuvio** erupted, the town was covered in volcanic mud, more than 36 feet deep in places. This helped preserve the wooden beams, doors and windows of the two-story houses. The first discovery at Herculaneum was accidental. Part of the theater was found when a well was being dug in 1709. Uncovering of the town began in 1828, but only in 1927, under Mussolini, did systematic excavation start.

A wall painting in a house at Herculaneum

*A view of the forum in Pompeii looking toward **Vesuvio**.*

The bodies of some Pompeians, who died during the eruption, have been preserved because they were enveloped by ash. As the bodies decayed, a kind of mold in the shape of the human form was left. These natural molds were found when Pompeii was excavated, and plaster casts were made from them.

The excavations at Pompeii and Herculaneum have provided valuable evidence about the way of life at the time. By examining the objects found in the ruins, archeologists have worked out where the commercial and residential areas were.

Pompeii was much larger than Herculaneum, with about 25,000 people. An earthquake in AD 63 had done considerable damage to the town, but the AD 79 eruption destroyed it completely. A 18-foot layer of burning ash and cinders covered the town. The ash at Pompeii was relatively easy to dig through, but the heat of it had burnt away wood and other perishable material.

Pompeii was rediscovered in the 16th century, but it was only in 1748 that systematic excavation began. It revealed:
– the Temple of Apollo
– the forum, Temple of Jupiter and Arch of Caligula
– villas with their wall frescoes and mosaic floors. The paintings usually have a red background.
– cobbled streets paved with polygonal stones

– large stones to restrict wheeled traffic, and for people to step across flooded streets. (You can see the ruts made by chariot wheels.)
– water towers at most crossroads
– shops with their signs
– public baths, three theaters and a stadium (where visiting fans were killed during a crowd riot in AD 53).

*Approaching the summit of **Vesuvio**, you can see where the vegetation stops, and the lava flows from the last eruption in 1944 begin. You have to pay for a guide, who is supposed to accompany you. The inside walls of the crater fall away in a precipitous drop, but the view out over il Golfo di Napoli is magnificent.*

La cucina italiana

Specialità regionali

Mangiare bene (eating well) is a way of life in Italy. In la cucina italiana (Italian cooking), every region has its own specialità (specialties) of which local people are very proud.

Le specialità are often made with the food products most easily available in that region. Pizza, from Napoli and the south, started out as inexpensive but sustaining food—a dough base covered with tomatoes, mozzarella and anchovies, with a sprinkling of oregano.

Polenta comes from **le Alpi**. It is made from maize flour, water and a little salt. This dish provides something warm and filling for people in the harsh mountain winters. It is served with Fontina cheese (which melts into long strings) or with meat or a sauce.

Risotti (rice dishes) are associated

Osso buco

with **la Valle Padana** in northern Italy where rice is a major crop. For **un risotto**, short-grain rice is cooked with ingredients, like **funghi** (mushrooms) or **gamberetti** (shrimps). The most famous is **il risotto alla milanese**, cooked with saffron, browned onion and rosemary. **Milano** also has **carni** (meat dishes) like **cotoletta alla milanese** (veal chop covered in breadcrumbs before frying) and **osso buco** (veal stew).

Traditionally, **Emilia Romagna** has some of the finest food in Italy. For this reason, **il capoluogo** Bologna is called **la Grassa** (the fat one). **Specialità** include: pork products such as **salame**, **mortadella**, **salsiccia**, **zampone** (pigs' feet); **tortellini** (pasta rings stuffed with pork); **prosciutto di Parma** (Parma or raw ham); **parmigiano** (Parmesan cheese), and **vitello alla bolognese** (veal cooked with Parma ham and cheese). The meat sauce for **spaghetti bolognese** comes from Bologna, but Italians usually call it **il ragù**.

Among **specialità** from **Roma** are: **gnocchi alla romana** (made of semolina, mozzarella and **parmigiano**), and **saltimbocca** (slices of veal with **prosciutto** and sage). **Saltimbocca** means 'jump in the mouth'.

As well as pizza, one of **le specialità** from **Napoli** is **bistecca alla pizzaiola** (pizzaman's steak)—cooked in a sauce made of fresh tomatoes and oregano, with a slice of melting mozzarella on top. **Spaghetti alla napoletana** has a sauce made of tomatoes.

From all over Italy there are many **pesci** (fish) and **frutti di mare** (seafood) dishes. In **Puglia**, try **zuppa di cozze** (mussel soup with white wine and tomatoes), or **ostriche** (fresh oysters baked with breadcrumbs). Typical fish from the sea around **Calabria**, **Sicilia** and **Sardegna** are **sardine** (sardines), **acciughe** (anchovies), **tonno** (tuna), and **pesce spada** (swordfish). **La burrida**, a kind of fish stew, is **una specialità della Sardegna**.

Salame

Most beef (il manzo) comes from la Pianura Padana. Beef from Piemonte is considered very good, so you may find una macelleria piemontese a long way from this region.

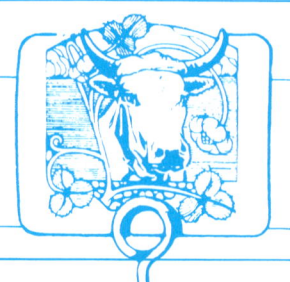

Cosa vuole bere?

When you want something to drink, try some typical Italian soft drinks:

- **un chinotto** (looks like cola, but has a sour orange flavor)
- **un'orzata** (sweet barley drink)
- **una menta** (peppermint flavor)
- **una granita** (crushed ice and syrup which comes in flavors like **al limone**, **alla menta** and **al caffè**)
- **acqua minerale**, bottled mineral water which comes **gassata** (fizzy) or **non gassata** (flat)
- **una spremuta d'arancia** (fresh orange juice)

Lo sapevate . . . ?

✳ A lemonade is **una gazzosa**. **Una limonata** is a drink made with freshly squeezed lemon juice and water.

Una tazza di caffè?

For Italians, **un caffè** is a small cup of very strong coffee made from freshly ground coffee beans. It is also known as **un espresso**.

Here are some other ways Italians drink coffee:

caffè ristretto – even stronger than usual
caffè macchiato – with a dash of milk
caffè lungo – with some water added (still strong)
caffè corretto – with liquor, often **grappa**
caffè con panna – with whipped cream
cappuccino – a large cup of coffee with hot frothy milk
caffelatte – a bowl of hot milk with coffee

*Above: Fish can be bought fresh at fishing ports all over Italy. **Tonno** steaks are often grilled with white wine and olive oil.*

*Left: Olive (olives) are used in many dishes. You can buy **olive nere** or **olive verdi**.*

Wine making in Italy goes back more than 2,500 years to Roman times. Some of the best known wines are:

I vini rossi (red):

Barolo and **Barbaresco**: From **Piemonte**, these wines are often served with **un arrosto** (roast meat) or **carne alla griglia** (a grill).
Chianti: From **Toscana**, one of Italy's best known wines.
Marsala: A sweet dessert wine from **Sicilia**.
Valpolicella: A lighter red wine from **Veneto**.

I vini bianchi (white):

Asti Spumante: From **Piemonte**, Italy's equivalent of champagne.
Frascati: Honey-colored wine from **i Colli Albani** near **Roma**.
Orvieto: From **Umbria**, a light dessert wine.
Soave: From Verona in the **Veneto** and bottled in slim, green bottles, it is often served with fish.

BARBARESCO
DENOMINAZIONE DI ORIGINE CONTROLLATA E GARANTITA

RISERVA
1982
VIGNETI IN
MOCCAGATTA

DI QUESTA RISERVA SONO STATE PRODOTTE 20325 BOTTIGLIE
QUESTA È LA N⁰ 20190

IMBOTTIGLIATO ALL'ORIGINE DAI
PRODUTTORI del BARBARESCO
Soc. Coop. r.l. - BARBARESCO · Italia

High-quality wines from a specific area that are made from certain grapes are labeled DOC (Denominazione di Origine Controllata).

This label for Barbaresco shows that only a limited number of bottles were produced—20,325.

■ *What number does this label have?*

Lo sapevate . . . ?

Paninoteche – Fast food

✳ Italy's version of fast food is pizza. **Gli hamburgher** are a recent introduction. You're unlikely to find them outside the larger towns and cities. Many of the items on the menu in hamburger restaurants are called by English names, because it is considered more fashionable.

In Italia si mangia bene!

A casa (at home), **la colazione** is usually **caffelatte** or **cappuccino** (coffee), **pane** (bread) and **marmellata** (jam or marmalade). Some people have coffee and a pastry or a croissant in a cafe or bar near where they work.

Although Italians don't eat much for **la colazione**, they make up for it later. Many people still get a two-hour (or more) lunch break and eat a three-course meal for **pranzo** and **cena**. In the cities, many large companies now have **l'orario continuato** (continuous working hours). With **il continuato**, people have an hour for lunch, but they were used to a longer break, so they call it continuous working. Those with a long lunch break usually go back home for lunch. Their homes are only a short distance away. Commuting over long distances is not very popular.

Meal times vary depending on **la regione**. **Un milanese** may have **il pranzo** at 12.30 or 1.00, while **un romano** will eat an hour or so later. **La cena** is also eaten earlier (from 7 p.m. on) in the north than the south.

These are the different courses of an Italian meal:

Antipasto
This starts the meal and includes items like **prosciutto crudo** (raw ham) with melon, **insalata di mare** (seafood salad), or mozzarella cheese served with raw tomatoes.

Primo piatto
Il primo piatto (first course) can be either a pasta dish, **una minestra** (soup), or **un risotto**.

Il secondo piatto
Il secondo piatto or **pietanza** (main course) of **carne** (meat) or **pesce** (fish) is always accompanied by **un contorno** (side dish of vegetables or salad), which is often served on a separate plate.

Pizza is a main course, but it is often eaten as a light meal (with a dessert), or as a snack (**uno spuntino**).

Dolce o frutta
Dessert is usually **frutta** (fresh fruit). If people have **dolce**—a piece of cake, creme caramel or mousse—it is served before **la frutta**.

If cheese forms part of a meal, it comes after **il secondo piatto**, but before the dessert.

PRANZO	
Antipasto	Prosciutto e melone
Primo	Maccheroni al pomodoro
Secondo	Cotoletta alla milanese
Contorno	Patate fritte
	Insalata mista
Dolce	Budino al cioccolato

Look at the lunch menu above and some English descriptions of these dishes below. Which do you think go together?

A French fries
B Macaroni with tomato sauce
C Chocolate mousse
D Mixed salad
E Fried breaded veal chop
F Ham and melon

MENU' DELLO SCIATORE

* Antipasto
* Primo
* Secondo
* Dessert
* Bevande

£15.000

Alla pensione ristorante
LA PROVINCIALE
a 50 mt. dalle piste !

Frazione Melezet, 97 - ☎ 99164
BARDONECCHIA

- What kind of customer is this fixed-price menu aimed at?
- **Bevande** are also included. What do you think they are?

I formaggi italiani

There are more than 450 different Italian cheeses. Some of them you already know: **il parmigiano** (Parmesan cheese), a hard cheese which is grated to put over pasta dishes; **la mozzarella** is a soft cheese used for pizza. Originally, **mozzarella** was made from buffalo milk (**mozzarella di bufala**), but now it is more likely to be made from cow's milk.

Some other cheeses are:

Ricotta: a soft cheese used as a filling for pasta (**tortelloni**), in sauces or desserts.
Gorgonzola: a strong-flavored blue cheese which has been produced in Italy, since the 11th century.
Pecorino: a hard cheese often used instead of **il parmigiano**.

- What is the name of this cheese?
- Is it made from cow's milk or buffalo milk?

Le buone maniere

1 il coltello
2 la forchetta
3 il cucchiaio
4 il piatto
5 il tovagliolo
6 il bicchiere
7 il sale
8 il pepe
9 l'olio
10 l'aceto
11 il pane

What's different?
- You make your own salad dressing with **l'olio** (olive oil) and **l'aceto** (vinegar) that's on the table.
- The waiter will bring **il parmigiano** (grated Parmesan cheese) to sprinkle over pasta dishes or soup.
- Sometimes, there will be no pepper on the table. It will be brought to you if the food you are eating requires it.
- Italians can't eat a meal without **il pane** (bread), so you will always find some on the table. You may also find **grissini** (bread sticks) with the bread.

Lo sapevate . . . ?

* When you're sitting at table with other people in Italy, it is very likely someone may wish you **Buon appetito** (Enjoy your meal). You should reply **Altrettanto** (And you, too).

Pastamania
Do you know how to eat spaghetti?

The correct way to eat spaghetti is to mix up the sauce and the spaghetti with your fork. Catch a couple of strands of spaghetti on the end of your fork and wind them round the fork. You can push the end of the fork against the plate to prevent the spaghetti slipping off.

Pasta, a basic dough mixture, is made into hundreds of different shapes. Names are given according to the shape—**farfalle** (butterflies), **fettuccine** or **tagliatelle** (ribbons), **penne** (quill pens), **spaghetti** (strings), **cannelloni** (tubes).

The best pasta is **casalinga** (homemade). If you see this word on a menu, it means that the pasta is freshly made. Sometimes, egg is added which makes the pasta more yellow, or spinach which gives a green color. Pasta should be cooked **al dente**—until it is not too soft or too hard. Pasta goes soggy if it is cooked too long.

Lo sapevate . . . ?

* **Spaghetti alla carbonara** is a recent invention. At the end of World War II, **Roma** was full of American soldiers sent there to help free Italy from German occupation. The soldiers came up with the idea of mixing bacon and eggs with spaghetti. The recipe soon became popular with **i romani**.

* **I romani** have a reputation for eating a lot of pasta. Don't be surprised in **Roma**, if you're offered a plate of pasta big enough for two!

Eating out

Pizzerie range from places that serve only pizza to those with a full menu like **un ristorante**.

Una trattoria has a more informal atmosphere than **un ristorante** and is often cheaper. Sometimes a restaurant is called after the owner. This one is **da Remigio** which means 'at Remigio's'.

Even in northern Italy, in the evening you won't find restaurants open before 7.00 or 7.30 p.m.

In city centers, there are self-service restaurants and tavole calde, with ready-prepared hot or cold dishes. You don't have to have a full meal, and you won't pay a cover charge.

This restaurant is also **una pizzeria**. Most restaurants close one day a week. This one is closed on Mondays.
■ What kind of food does the restaurant specialize in?

In many restaurants, you'll find a **pane e coperto** (bread and cover) charge on the bill. There is also **servizio** (a service charge). When you pay for a meal or buy something, Italian law requires that you are given a receipt—**una ricevuta fiscale**. This is why a waiter or store assistant may insist you take your receipt.

Look at the bill for two people. Note how Italians write the figure 1, so that it looks almost like a 7.

To differentiate 7 from 1, the figure 7 is written with a bar across it, e.g. 7.
■ How much did **i primi piatti** cost?
■ Did both people have a side dish of vegetables or salad?
■ Did they have a dessert?
■ Did they drink any wine?

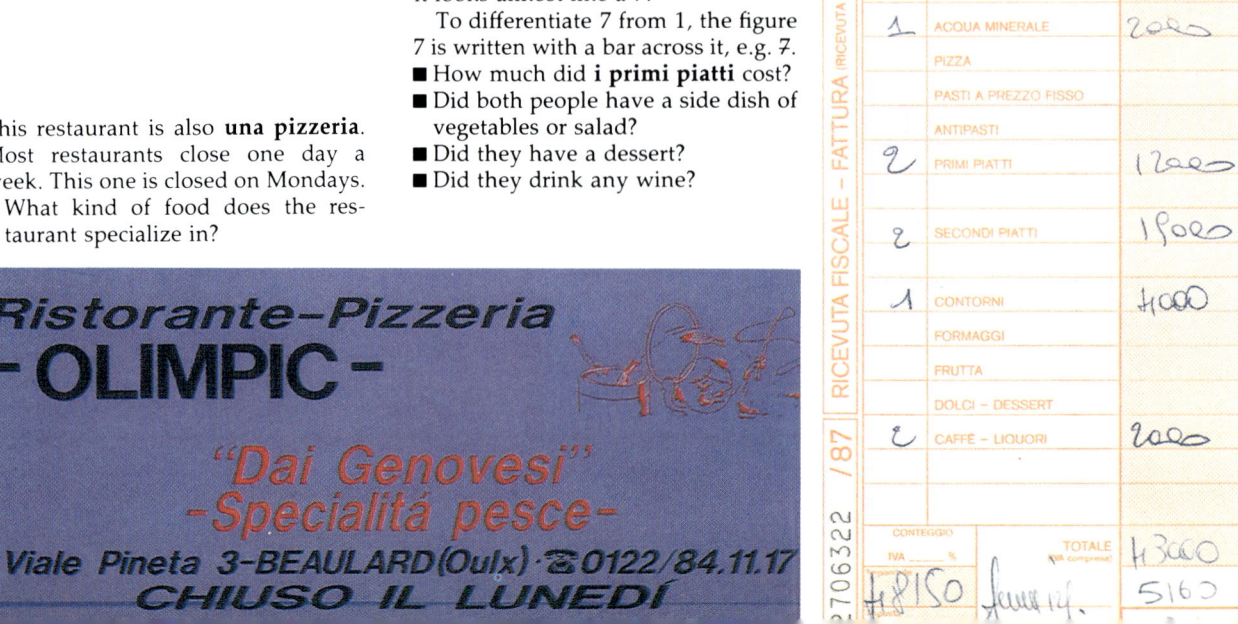

Quantità	Descrizione	Importo
2	COPERTI	4000
	VINO – BIRRA	
1	ACQUA MINERALE	2000
	PIZZA	
	PASTI A PREZZO FISSO	
	ANTIPASTI	
2	PRIMI PIATTI	12000
2	SECONDI PIATTI	19000
1	CONTORNI	4000
	FORMAGGI	
	FRUTTA	
	DOLCI – DESSERT	
2	CAFFÈ – LIQUORI	2000

Come si dice?

Waiter: Hello. What would you like?
Customer: I'd like **un antipasto misto**.

Waiter: And for your first course?
Customer: Mmm...I'd like **spaghetti alla napoletana**.

Waiter: And for your main course?
Customer: Veal escalope in Marsala wine sauce.

Waiter: What vegetables?
Customer: French fries and a green salad.

Waiter: Anything to drink?
Customer: A half-bottle of fizzy mineral water.

Waiter: Anything else? A dessert?
Customer: No. A coffee please...and the bill.

All'aperto

PANINI
FRULLATI
TRAMEZZINI
CREME CALDE
SPREMUTE
CAFFÈ CON PANNA
PANNA
CAFFÈ FREDDO
FRAPPÈ
T È FREDDO
CIOCCOLATA PANNA
BIRRA ALLA SPINA

Bars and cafés also sell **tramezzini** (sandwiches), like **un toast** (a toasted ham and cheese sandwich), or **panini** (rolls or sandwiches with different fillings).

Standing at the counter is cheaper than sitting at a table. If you want to sit and watch the world go by for a while, it may be worthwhile to spend the extra money and enjoy being **all'aperto** (in the open air) on the café terrace.

■ What two hot drinks can you have with whipped cream?
■ Which two drinks, which are usually served hot, can you have cold?

I signori clienti sono pregati di ritirare lo scontrino alla cassa.

If you see this sign on a café counter, you have to go to the cashier and pay for your drink or snack in advance. The cashier will give you **uno scontrino** (a ticket or receipt) which you give to the waiter at the counter. The waiter tears **lo scontrino** (to show s/he has served you) and gives it back to you as a receipt.

```
CANTINA DI TONY
V. EMANUELE 15
MONTEROSSO (SP)
P.I.00237460118
    I T A L I A

    0           n
D.01          5 000
CONTANTE      5 000
    2       10-09-88
/MFBB  6120991
```

Uno scontrino

Come si dice?

Cameriere!	Waiter!
Cosa desidera?	What would you like?
Quant'è?	How much is it?
Il conto, per piacere.	The bill, please.
Grazie.	Thank you.
Prego.	You're welcome.

Money matters

Lots of lire!

The money used in Italy is **la lira**. When people give prices, they talk about **lire**. Look at this photo of apples and oranges for sale in an Italian market. You'll see that the prices look high—in thousands of **lire**.

To simplify matters, the Italians are going to introduce a new lira which will be the equivalent of 1,000 old **lire**. For example, the largest note in circulation, which is 100,000 **lire**, would buy the same amount of goods, but it would be called 100 new lire.

There are notes of 1,000, 5,000, 10,000, 50,000, and 100,000 **lire**. The coins are 5, 10, 20, 50, 100, 200, and 500 lire. You're unlikely to find 5- or 10-lire coins, as they are being gradually withdrawn. In your change, you'll find mostly 100-, 200- or 500-lire coins.

Banks open Monday to Friday from 8.30 a.m. to 1.30 p.m. They also open for another hour in the afternoon, but this changes depending where you are.

Come si dice?

Buongiorno. Si cambiano qui i traveler's cheques.

Sì signorina. Quanto desidera cambiare?

Vorrei cambiare 20 dollari.

Girl: Hello. Do you change traveler's checks here?
Bank clerk: Yes, miss. How much would you like to change?
Girl: I'd like to change $20.

Ha il passaporto?

Eccolo.

Ed ecco la cassa.

Bank clerk: Passport, please?   Girl: Here it is.
Bank clerk: And the cashier is there.

You can change money in banks, or in **un cambio** (a money exchange).
Always check:
– the exchange rate (**il tasso di cambio**) before you change any money to see where you can obtain the best rate.
– how much Italian money you have been given. With so many zeros, it can be very confusing. The same applies for any change you are given in shops or cafés.

Lo sapevate . . . ?

* Metric measures are used in Italy. Food items like fruit or fish are sold by **il chilo** (the kilo), abbreviated to **kg**. For smaller items like **prosciutto**, ask for **un etto** which is 100 grams or 1/10th of **un chilo**.

■ What is strange about the way kilo is spelled on the price card for the strawberries?

Where can I buy . . . ?

Una salumeria sells cold meats and various delicatessen products. *Una rosticceria* sells ready-cooked meat, mainly chickens.

Bread is bought by *l'etto* or *il chilo* at *una panetteria*, where some **paste** (pastries) and cakes are also sold. If you want fresh, delicious pastries, go to *una pasticceria*. *Le paste* are sold *a peso* (by weight).

If you go to eat at someone's house, it's the custom to take some **paste fresche** (fresh cakes).

*Una latteria (from **latte** = milk) is a store which stocks dairy products as well as biscuits and some soft drinks. Milk is sold in bottles and cartons of **un litro** (a liter).*

*A general grocery store has an **alimentari** or **alimentazione** sign. There are not as many **supermercati** in Italy as in other countries, and they are mainly found away from city centers.*

■ What else does this store sell?

■ What is sold in these stores? ▶

*At **una farmacia** (pharmacy) only medicines and health-related products are sold. If you want cosmetics you have to go to **una profumeria**.*

Some other stores:

macelleria	butcher's shop
fruttivendolo	fruit and vegetable shop
pescheria	fish shop
(negozio di) calzature	shoe store
libreria	book and stationery store (note: **una biblioteca** is a library)

*All over Italy, you'll find **mercati rionali** (open-air markets) that sell food and sometimes clothes.*

Open or closed?

Shops open between 8:30 and 9:00 a.m. and close for lunch at 12:30 or 1:00 p.m. They re-open at 3:30 or 4:00 p.m. until 7:30 or 8:00 p.m. In northern cities, like **Milano, Torino** and **Venezia**, the lunch break is shorter and shops close earlier.

lunedì	Monday
martedì	Tuesday
mercoledì	Wednesday
giovedì	Thursday
venerdì	Friday
sabato	Saturday
domenica	Sunday

Shops are closed on Sundays. They also have **un riposo settimanale**, one day a week when they close. Look at this sign.

■ What are the Italian words for morning and afternoon?

◀ ■ This is a sign for a garage. When is it closed?

65

Going shopping

Elegantissimo!

Andare a vedere le vetrine a Milano

Fare bella figura (looking stylish) is as important as **mangiare bene** (eating well) to many Italians. They like to keep up with **la moda** (the latest fashion).

All large towns and cities have a street where you can window shop for the latest fashion. Shoppers often prefer to go to smaller boutiques where they get more individual attention. In **Roma**, **la via Condotti** has many elegant fashion shops. In **Milano**, try **andare a vedere le vetrine** (going window-shopping) in **la via Montenapoleone**.

Many Italian fashion names, like Fiorucci, Gucci, Ferragamo, and Benetton, are known throughout the world. **Milano** is the capital of Italian haute couture and ready-made clothes. If you buy clothes in Italy, you may find that you are months ahead of the fashions at home.

You may find some English names used for items of clothing, like **i jeans**. But note that a jumper is **un pullover**, and a cardigan is **un golf**. Some fashion shops like to use English names. If the name sounds trendy, it doesn't matter if not all the customers can understand it!

Articoli di pelle (leather goods) such as **borsette** (purses), **cinture** (belts), **guanti** (gloves), and **scarpe** (shoes) are examples of Italian craftsmanship. Every year, 500 million pairs of shoes are exported.

There are few department stores, and they are mainly found in cities. Look for **La Rinascente**, **UPIM**, *and* **Standa**.

Come si dice?

Two people are trying on things in different stores. Follow the conversation diagram and find out **a)** if the shirt is too big, and **b)** if the shoes are too small.

Che cosa desidera?

Vorrei provare questa camicia.

Vorrei vedere queste scarpe.

Come va?

Non va bene. È troppo piccola. Ha qualcosa di più grande?

Va bene, grazie. Le prendo.

Some other useful words and phrases:

lungo/a	long
corto/a	short
(di) meno caro	less expensive
bello/a	nice, beautiful
troppo caro/a	too expensive
Mi piace/	I like it/them.
Mi piacciono	
Quanto fa?	How much altogether?

L'artigianato

Italian standards of craftsmanship are high. In advertising for high-quality items, you may often see the word **artigiano** (craftsman) or **artigianale** (made by craftsmen) used.

L'artigianato also refers to the traditional Italian crafts like:

la ceramica	pottery
vetri e cristalli	glass and crystal objects
intagli in legno	wood carvings
lavori in oro e argento	gold and silver work
pizzi	lace
oggetti di alabastro	alabaster ornaments

*In Volterra, in **la regione della Toscana**, there is a tradition of making ornaments and dishes from alabaster which goes back to the time of the Etruscans.*

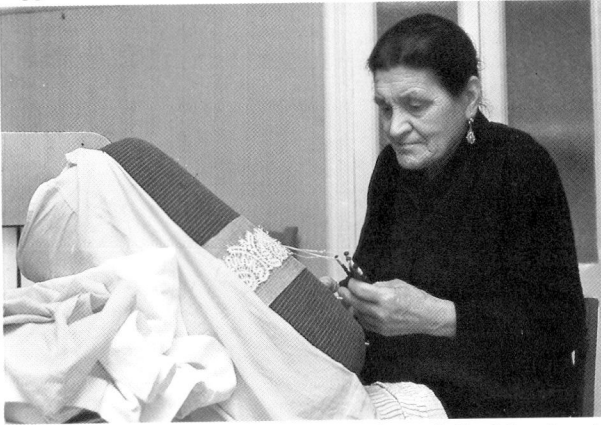

*This woman from Chieti, in **la regione delle Marche**, is making lace. Another traditional industry in the region is accordion making which is based in Castelfidardo.*

Lo sconto

Don't be shy about asking for **uno sconto** (a discount) when you buy something. You may not always know whether a particular store has such a policy, but it is quite acceptable to ask, especially when buying clothes.

Girl: How much is it?
Assistant: 110,000 lire.

Girl: 110,000 lire? That's a lot!
Assistant: Not really, miss.
Girl: Can I have a discount?

Usually, there are no discounts in food stores, but this store is offering an end-of-season reduction.
■ What discount can you get on a box of chocolates?

Assistant: Well, yes. . . let's say 100,000.
Girl: Thank you.

Assistant: I'm sorry. We don't give discounts. The prices are fixed.
Girl: I'll leave it, thanks.

Signs with **saldi** mean there's a sale on. This store is offering a special promotional sale.

Keeping in touch

Saluti da Napoli

If you're sending **cartoline** (post-cards), you have to pay the same rate as for **lettere** (letters), unless you put only a greeting and a signature on the card. You can buy **francobolli** (stamps) at . . .

. . . *la posta* . . .

■ How much does **una cartolina** cost?

Lo sapevate . . . ?

* Italian airmail envelopes have green and red stripes around the edges. Red, white and green are the colors of the Italian flag.

Come si dice?

◀ . . . or where you see this sign.

■ If you were in ▶ **Roma** and sending **una cartolina** abroad, which slot would you put it in?

Una cassetta postale (a mail box) is red.

Cinque francobolli per gli Stati Uniti, per favore.

Some other useful words and phrases:

un aerogramma	an air letter
per via aerea	by airmail

Da non perdere!

▷ Look for interesting stamps from **la Repubblica di San Marino** and **il Vaticano** to put on **cartoline** you send home. These independent states issue their own stamps.

■ Can you work out the Italian words for north, south, east, and west from this stamp?

Un francobollo della ▶ Repubblica di San Marino

Phoning home

The best place to make long distance calls is from **telefoni pubblici** (public phone offices). These are operated by SIP, the Italian state-owned telephone company.

Write down the town, the country and the number you want. Give this to the operator who will place the call for you. You pay for the call when you've finished. It usually costs less than calling from your hotel, unless your hotel has a pay phone.

To use a pay phone, buy **gettoni** (tokens). These are worth 200 lire each. You can get these from **la posta** (the post office), from **un chiosco di giornali** (a newspaper stand), or wherever you see the **Tabacchi** sign. Make sure you get a lot of **gettoni** for a long distance call. You can always change **gettoni** back into Italian money in your hotel. Occasionally, you may find someone gives you **un gettone** in your change.

■ As well as **gettoni**, what other coins can you use in this pay phone?

Un gettone

Some pay phones now take **una scheda telefonica** (a phonecard). They are handy if you have a lot of calls to make. You can buy **schede** worth 3,000, 6,000 or 10,000 lire.

Some phrases that may be useful:

introdurre gettoni e/o monete   put in **gettoni** and/or coins
sganciare il microtelefono   lift the receiver
comporre il numero   dial the number
premere il tasto rosso/giallo   press the red/yellow button.
è occupato   it's busy
riagganciare il microtelefono   hang up
fuori servizio   out of order

Lo sapevate . . . ?

✻ The cheapest time to make international phone calls is between 10 p.m. and 8 a.m.

■ What is the value of this phonecard?

Help!

If you need to call the police or an ambulance, the emergency number is 113. The loss or theft of valuable items should be reported to the police immediately. Make sure you have a copy of the police report for your insurance company.

Ho perso tutti i soldi.

la macchina fotografica

le lenti a contatto

i traveler's checks

i soldi

il passaporto

La Chiesa cattolica

Most Italians are Catholics, although they may not all practice their religion regularly. Italians often feel that **la Chiesa cattolica** (the Roman Catholic Church) is 'their' church, because its center has been in **Roma** for so long.

Especially in smaller towns, **il parroco** (the parish priest) is an influential person. People often ask **il parroco** for a personal reference when applying for a job.

Chiara is 21, and she will soon take her final vows as a nun. When she left school at 18, she spent a year in a community of nuns so that she knew what life as a nun would be like. After that she began her two-year training to become a member of the Franciscan-Elizabethan order. This order helps run centers for people who are handicapped, drug addicts, prostitutes, and single mothers. There are also missions in Africa and Latin America to which Chiara might be sent. Chiara wanted to become a nun so that she could dedicate herself to God and help others.

Il Vaticano

For nearly 2,000 years, **la Chiesa cattolica** (the Roman Catholic Church) has been based in **Roma**. **Il Papa** (the pope), the head of the Church, is also head of **la città del Vaticano**, an independent state in the heart of the capital. The independence of the Vatican state was officially recognized by the Italian government under the Lateran Treaties of 1929. Just like any other state, **il Vaticano** sends ambassadors abroad.

◄ *Until 1970, il Vaticano had its own armed forces. Now only the Swiss Guard remains. It has served in the Vatican for over 400 years. The soldiers still stand guard in their yellow, blue and red uniforms, said to have been designed by Michelangelo.*

Il Vaticano has its own flag, currency, postage stamps, radio station, and newspaper, *l'Osservatore Romano*. Fewer than 1,000 people live inside the 109-acre city.

radio vaticana

GIOVEDI' 18	
7.20-17.30-23.20: Orizzonti Cristiani	**20.40:** Recita del S. Rosario
7.30: Santa Messa Latina	**21.10-23:** Radiovaticanasera, quotidiano d'attualità
8-12.30-17: Quattrovoci	**21.30:** Aux sources de la musique
14.30: Radiogiornale in italiano, spagnolo, portoghese, francese, inglese, tedesco e polacco	**21.50:** Vatican Wiew Point
	22.10: Mesa Redonda. Temas a debate
16.30: Gli anniversari: Leonard Bernstein	**24:** Studio A (Con voi nella notte)

■ Why do you think there are program names in English, Spanish and French, as well as Italian?

Every Sunday crowds come to St. Peter's Square to hear the pope's message. On la domenica di Pasqua (Easter Sunday), thousands gather for the pope's blessing. The present pope, il Papa Giovanni Paolo II, was the first non-Italian pope to be elected for 456 years. He comes from Poland. Since he became pope, he has traveled thousands of miles to visit the world's 700 million Catholics.

This 100-lire coin is from **il Vaticano**, but you can use it anywhere in Italy. On one side is the Vatican coat of arms. These also appear on the Vatican flag.

■ Why do you think there is a dove on this side?

At this 12-century monastery at Pràglia, near **Pàdova (Padua)**, the Benedictine monks lead a simple life of hard work and prayer. They grow their own food and sell products such as wine, honey and . . . beauty creams! For centuries, monks from Pràglia have prepared medicines and ointments using ingredients like herbs and honey.

Some monasteries became centers for wine production because in time of war, they were left relatively untouched by the warring armies.

Le feste

Natale: Christmas is very much a family occasion, although some people go out to a restaurant. Many restaurants are open on Christmas Day. There is no set Christmas meal, but **panettone**, a special cake, is eaten at Christmas time. Traditionally, presents are brought by an old woman called Befana. Children are told that, if they don't behave well, Befana won't bring them presents.

Il Capodanno: Italians ring in the New Year with **il veglione di San Silvestro**. Restaurants are booked up months in advance for groups of family and friends.

Pasqua:

Carnevale is held all over Italy before the start of **la quaresima** (Lent), the 40-day period leading up to **la domenica di Pasqua** (Easter Sunday). A dove-shaped cake called **colomba** is eaten at **Pasqua**.

Il compleanno: As well as birthdays, a person's name day (**l'onomastico**) is sometimes celebrated. **L'onomastico** comes on the day dedicated to the saint after whom a person is named.

Il battesimo: A christening is a big family affair. Parents choose two godparents, **il padrino** (godfather) and **la madrina** (godmother), for their baby. After the ceremony, everyone goes for a celebratory meal in a restaurant—even the baby!

La prima comunione: First Communion at the age of seven or eight is an important stage in a child's life. Girls often wear expensive dresses that look like mini-wedding dresses, while boys wear suits or a white monk's habit.

Il matrimonio: No expense is spared. **La sposa** (the bride) may spend over a million lire on her wedding dress. **Gli sposi** (newlyweds) receive expensive presents, including items like color televisions or washing machines. The reception often lasts from lunch until evening. An orchestra or a disco may be hired for guests to dance to.

Most people marry in church. The Church now organizes **corsi per fidanzati** (courses for engaged couples) to make them more aware of the meaning of marriage.

Lo sapevate . . . ?

✶ For Italians, **confetti** are sugared almonds in small boxes which are given at **un matrimonio**, **un battesimo** and **una prima comunione**. At weddings, people throw uncooked rice.

Lo sport

Il calcio

Il calcio (soccer) is a national passion. The results of **partite** (matches) played every Sunday are discussed at length in homes and cafés all over the country.

Star players are bought and sold for huge amounts of money, a few even for millions of dollars. The money invested in such players means that every aspect of their lives, on and off the field, is carefully examined in sports newspapers and magazines.

The national team plays in blue and so is often called **la squadra azzurra**.

Some of the best-known teams in **la Serie A** (the top league) are given nicknames according to the team colors:

i rossoneri	**AC Milan**
i bianconeri	**Juventus** (from **Torino**)
gli azzurri	**Napoli**
i nerazzurri	**Inter** (from **Milano**)
i giallorossi	**Roma**

■ Which of these colors do you already know? Use a dictionary to find out those you don't know.

Tifosi (fans) like to show exactly which team they support. These **tifosi** support **AC Milan**.

This newspaper clipping shows the results of a survey about which team Italians think will win **la Serie A**. (1 = **Napoli** will win; X = **Napoli** and **AC Milan** will draw; 2 = **AC Milan** will win.)

■ In the over-60 age group more people think **Napoli** will win. What does the 15–24 age group think?

■ In the right hand column what kind of categories are used to classify people's opinions?

Misuriamo giorno per giorno l'umore della gente

I sondaggi «Gazzetta»

Napoli-Milan
L'Italia vota così

I sessantenni credono nel Napoli	1	X	2
15-24 anni	37	23	40
25-44	47	22	31
45-60	45	19	36
oltre 60	50	16	34

Gli studenti danno fiducia al Milan	1	X	2
Studenti	19	25	56
Impiegati	54	13	32
Professionisti	58	17	25
Casalinghe	31	31	38
Operai	36	19	45
Artigiani	62	15	23

■ How did **a)** students, and **b)** housewives (**casalinghe**) vote?

Altri sport

Il ciclismo is a popular amateur and professional sport. The most important professional race is **il Giro d'Italia** which lasts three weeks. It is considered the second most difficult cycle race in the world after the Tour de France. **Il Giro** includes tough mountain stages in **le Alpi**.

Ciclisti in una corsa di bicicletta ▶

In **i motori** (motor racing) **le rosse** means Ferrari. Enzo Ferrari (1898–1988) raced for Alfa Romeo before starting his own company. Over the last 40 years Ferrari has won more world championships and produced more world champions than any other team.

The Ferrari **scudetto** (badge) has a black horse. This was the badge of World War I air ace Francesco Baracca in whose air force squadron Enzo Ferrari served.

The two Grand Prix circuits are: Monza, near **Milano**, and Imola near Bologna.

Some other sports popular in Italy:

il tennis	tennis
il basket	basketball
la pallavolo	volleyball
l'equitazione	show jumping (also means horseback riding)
l'ippica	horse racing
il ping pong	table tennis
la scherma	fencing
la vela	sailing
il nuoto	swimming
le bocce	bowling (a traditional sport played on gravel or sand)

■ Practice asking and saying which sport you like watching or doing the most.

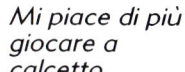

Quale sport Le piace di più?

Mi piace di più guardare la vela.

Mi piace di più giocare a calcetto.

This is a poster for the 30th Baseball World Championships being held in Italy. Baseball is not usually associated with Italy, but Italy has one of the best national teams in Europe.

There are two baseball leagues. The teams are mainly from northern towns—Parma, Novara, Grosseto, Bologna, **Milano**, and **Torino**, although there is one from **Roma**.

■ What is the Italian for world championship?

Free time

Vediamo un film?

If you'd like to see **un film**, you can watch it **alla tivù** (on TV) or **al cine** (at the movies). Italians are frequent moviegoers. Italy produces its own films, but films from other countries are also shown. Foreign films are usually **doppiati** (dubbed) into Italian.

There are three state-owned television **canali** (channels)—**Raiuno**, **Raidue**, and **Raitre**. These are run by **RAI (Radio Televisione Italiana)**. In addition, there are private television stations which show a lot of advertising (much more than the state channels), and have commercial sponsors for programs. No one is quite sure how many private stations there are, because new ones start up all the time.

Canali privati

Here are some of the programs you'll find **alla tivù** (on TV):

attualità	current affairs
varietà	variety/light entertainment
gioco	game show
quiz	quiz show
sceneggiato	mini-series
teleromanzo/telenovella	soap opera
telefilm	series
musica	music
documentario	documentary
notizie	news
cartoni animati	cartoons

■ Can you say in Italian what kind of programs you like?

This film was directed by Bernardo Bertolucci. The chief cameraman was also Italian—Vittorio Storaro. Many top Italian cameramen work on foreign films.

■ What is the English title of this film?

Il collezionista

Some people like **fare collezione** (to collect something) in their spare time. This **collezionista** has made his **cinquecento** (Fiat 500) into a moving display of **decalcomanie** (stickers).
■ Do you collect anything?

Faccio collezione di. . .

. . .cartoline.

●RAIUNO ‖‖‖‖‖

7.15 Attualità: Unomattina.
9.35 Varietà: «Dadaumpa». Una storia del varietà televisivo.
10.30 TG 1 mattina.
10.40 Attualità: Intorno a noi. Con Giosué Boetto e Sabina Ciuffini.
11.30 Sceneggiato: «Michele Strogoff» (9ª puntata).
11.55 Che tempo fa.
12.00 TG 1 - Flash.
12.05 Varietà: «Pronto... è la Rai?». Con Giancarlo Magalli e Simona Marchini.
13.30 Telegiornale.
13.55 Attualità: «TG 1, tre minuti di...».
14.15 Documenti: «Il mondo di Quark». I serpenti di mare; la donnola e l'ermellino.
15.00 Attualità: Cronache italiane.
15.30 Attualità: TG 1 - Cronache. Nord chiama Sud, Sud chiama Nord.

16.00 Varietà: «Big». Conduce Pippo Franco.
17.35 Attualità: «Spaziolibero».
17.55 Oggi al Parlamento.
18.00 TG 1 - Flash.
18.05 Gioco: «Parola mia». Conduce Luciano Rispoli. Con Anna Carlucci.
19.30 Attualità: «Un libro, un amico».
19.40 Almanacco del giorno dopo.
20.00 Telegiornale.
20.30 Attualità: «Il caso». Conduce Enzo Biagi.
21.45 Film: «Ehi amico... c'è Sabata, hai chiuso!» (western, Italia, 1969). Regia di Frank Kramer (Gian Franco Pavolini). Con Lee Van Cleef, William Berger. Nell'intervallo (ore 22.45): Telegiornale.
23.40 ● PALLANUOTO - Amichevole: Italia-Germania Ovest (sintesi da Firenze).
24.00 TG1 - Notte.
0.15 Documenti: «Laboratorio Infanzia».

Look at these programs on a state-owned channel.
■ What is unusual about the western at 9:45 p.m.?
■ What English word is used for the news bulletins at noon and 6 p.m.?
■ Which program gives information about the Italian parliament?
■ What time is the weather report on?

Che cosa sta leggendo?

In Italy, **giornali** (newspapers) with large circulations are still associated with **le regioni** where they were started.

*This paper is from **Milano** and was* ▶ *started in 1876. It is **un quotidiano** (a daily paper).*

Another **quotidiano** is *La Stampa* from **Torino**.
■ Can you find a local newspaper for **una regione** or **una città** that you have visited in Italy?

■ What special subject does this paper report on?

This **rivista** (magazine) is **un mensile** (a monthly) which has reports on popular music, films and TV.
■ Two posters are given away with the magazine. Which two singing stars appear on them? (One is Italian, the other American.)

Paninari are young people who wear only certain brands of jeans, baseball jackets and moccasin-style shoes. They meet at hamburger restaurants. Teenager Letizia Mottica has written a **paninaro** novel.

Many people think that the **paninaro** phenomenon is just another commercial gimmick to make young people spend their money.

Fa collezione di decalcomanie.

. . . maschere di carnevale.

*Fare un giro is popular with everyone. These girls are out for a ride on their **scooter** (scooters), and have stopped to pass the time of day with a friend. A lot of people in Italy ride **scooter** or **motorini** (mopeds) to school or to work.*

Lo sapevate . . . ?

✱ The scooter was invented by the Italians in 1944. The best known kind of Italian scooter is **la Vespa**.

Words and music

I bestseller

I PRIMI CINQUE

1 TUROW - **Presunto innocente**
Mondadori   p. 100

2 MARCHI - **Grandi peccatori grandi**
Rizzoli   **cattedrali**   73

3 MUSATTI - **Curar nevrotici con la propria**
Mondadori   **autoanalisi**   58

4 MANZONI - **I promessi sposi**
Le Monnier   45

5 ALIGHIERI - **Inferno**
La Nuova Italia   38

Books by many Italian writers, both old and new, are also available in English translation.

These are the results of a survey conducted by *La Stampa* to find out which were **i libri più venduti** (the bestselling books) during a week at the beginning of the school year.

At Number 4 is *I promessi sposi* by Alessandro Manzoni (1785–1873). Traditionally, it is a book studied by Italian children at school. When it was first published in 1827, the book sold so quickly it had to be reprinted nine times.

The fifth book on the list is part of the poem *La Divina Commedia* by Dante (1265–1321). The three parts of *La Divina Commedia—Inferno*, *Purgatorio* and *Paradiso*—describe the journey of a pilgrim through Hell, Purgatory and Heaven. Dante wrote the book in the everyday language of the people of **Firenze**, so that it could be understood by all. At that time, many books were written in Latin.

Stories in **fumetti** (cartoon strips) are popular. This book is a cartoon-strip history book.
- Which city's history does it cover?

Entrare in scena

From the 16th to the 18th century, **la commedia dell' arte** was Italy's 'street theater'. Italian traveling companies made **la commedia dell' arte** popular throughout Europe.

Certain stock characters, like the servant **Arlecchino** (Harlequin) and the merchant **Pantalone** (Pantaloon), appeared. The actors wore special masks and costumes to show the character they were playing. Each character spoke in a different **dialetto**. **Arlecchino** always had a multicolored diamond-patterned suit. Pulcinella had a large nose and spoke in **napoletano**. The young lovers always spoke in **fiorentino**.

The play was improvised around a plot called **uno scenario** which was decided on beforehand. The actors invented witty, sometimes satirical dialogue and jokes, played tricks on each other, and even performed acrobatics.

When the play **Sei personaggi in cerca d'autore** *(Six characters in search of an author) was first performed in* **Roma** *in 1921, it caused pandemonium in the theater. The playwright Luigi Pirandello (1867–1936) and his daughter had to leave through the stage door. Pirandello's plays disturbed people because they explored the way in which reality and illusion are linked. He was awarded the Nobel Prize for literature in 1934.*

LUIGI PIRANDELLO
1867–1936

Lire 40

✱ Although William Shakespeare probably never visited Italy, a number of his plays are set in Italy. These include *The Merchant of Venice, Julius Caesar, Two Gentlemen of Verona,* and *Othello.* Shakespeare's tragic young lovers, Romeo and Juliet, lived in Verona. In Italian, they are called **Giulietta e Romeo**.

L'opera

The origin of opera was in 16th-century Florentine **melodramma**, where words were sung rather than spoken, and the melody of the music, as well as the words, expressed feelings. The earliest opera still performed is *Orfeo*. It was written in 1607 for **il Carnevale di Mantova** (the Mantua Carnival) by composer Claudio Monteverdi.

Originally an entertainment for the nobility, opera was first performed in a commercial theater in **Venezia** in 1637. Opera became so popular that people would gather outside theaters in the hope of hearing some of the opera being performed. The best-loved arias were sung by everyone, and played at cafés.

The great composer Mozart was Austrian, but he worked with an Italian librettist, da Ponte. Many Mozart operas are sung in Italian—*Don Giovanni*, *Le nozze di Figaro* (*The Marriage of Figaro*), and *Così fan tutte*.

Among the most famous Italian opera composers are Verdi, Donizetti, Bellini, Rossini and Puccini.

Perhaps the most famous opera house in the world is **il Teatro alla Scala** in **Milano**. It was built between 1776 and 1778 and can hold an audience of 2,000 spectators.

This poster gives details of **un concerto di canto** (a song recital) by Italy's leading tenor Luciano Pavarotti.

After the premiere of Giuseppe Verdi's opera **Un ballo in maschera** (A Masked Ball) *in 1859, the audience in the Apollo Theater in* **Roma** *shouted,* "Viva Verdi!" *It had become a rallying cry for Italian patriots: V.E.R.D.I. stood for* **Vittorio Emanuele Re d' Italia** *(Victor Emmanuel King of Italy). Verdi's opera* **Nabucco** *had been banned by the Austrian police who then occupied* **Milano***, because a scene with a choir of captive Jews clearly symbolized the captivity of Italy.*

Verdi (1813–1901) also wrote **Rigoletto** *(1851), and* **La Traviata** *and* **Il Trovatore** *(1853). In 1869, he was commissioned to write an opera to celebrate the opening of the Suez Canal, for which he composed* **Aida**.

Every instrument in this photo was made by master craftsman **Antonio Stradivari** *(1644–1737) from Cremona. The photo was taken at a concert commemorating the 250th anniversary of his death.* **Stradivari** *and his sons made more than a thousand violins, violas and cellos, but only 600 of these* **stradivari** *still exist. No one knows exactly what gives these instruments their unique rich tone.*

The design of the modern violin was developed by Andrea Amati (c.1520–c.1578), also from Cremona. Amati's grandson taught **Stradivari** *and another great violin maker,* **Guarneri** *(d.1698), the art of violin making.*

The language of music is Italian. Many musical forms in Western classical music originated in Italy—**madrigale**, **concerto**, **opera**, and **sonata**. The custom of showing the **tempo**, the speed at which music should be played, started in Italy in the 16th century. Because Italian music was very popular all over Europe, the custom spread.

Some musical **tempi**:

– **allegro ma non troppo**	lively, but not too fast
– **andante**	literally means going. In music it means at a moderate pace
– **cantabile**	in a singing style
– **crescendo**	getting gradually louder

Italy in the world

Pionieri italiani

Here are some Italians who have made important contributions to the modern world:

Maria Montessori

Despite fierce opposition, Maria Montessori (1870–1952) became the first woman to receive a medical degree in Italy. From her work with mentally-handicapped children, she believed that some of her teaching methods could be equally useful for all young children. In 1907, she opened the first **casa dei bambini** (children's house) for young children in a Roman slum.

The success of her ideas about allowing each child to develop at its own pace, but at the same time stimulating it through special exercises and games attracted interest in Italy and other parts of the world. There are now Montessori nursery schools in countries all over the world. Many Montessori methods have also been adopted in modern nursery schools.

A Montessori school

Guglielmo Marconi

In 1895, Guglielmo Marconi (1874–1937) invented an apparatus for sending signals without connecting wires. He sent his 'wireless' message from his father's house at Pontecchio, near Bologna. By 1901, further experiments led to the first transatlantic radio transmission from Poldhu in Cornwall (Britain) to St. John's in Newfoundland (Canada). For his work, Marconi shared the Nobel Prize for Physics in 1909.

When the liner Titanic hit an iceberg and sank in the North Atlantic in 1912, many people were saved because other ships picked up the radio SOS call.

Marconi later worked on the development of microwave and shortwave radio transmission. The first microwave radio service was between **la Città del Vaticano** and the Pope's summer residence at Castel Gandolfo in 1933.

*The inventor Marconi is commemorated in the name of this **aliscafo** (hydrofoil) on **il lago di Como**. Numerous **aliscafo** services operate between Italian islands and the mainland, and on the lakes.*

*In 1906, Italian engineer Enrico Forlanini built the first hydrofoil to fly with its hull clear of the water. Italy is the world's second largest manufacturer of **aliscafi**.*

* The Americas were discovered by one Italian and named after another.

Genoese navigator **Cristoforo Colombo** (1451–1506) believed that the world was round, so that by sailing west he would eventually reach the East. Sponsored by the king and queen of Spain, he reached what he called the West Indies in 1492. On a third voyage in 1498, he reached the mainland of South America, although he thought that it was Asia.

Amerigo Vespucci (1454–1512) became interested in exploration when he was the Medici representative in Seville in Spain. In 1499, his expedition explored the northeast coast of South America and discovered the mouth of the Amazon. Because Vespucci claimed that he had discovered a 'new world', in 1507, a mapmaker called the new land America after the Latin version of Vespucci's name—*Americus Vespucius*.

Do you know the names of any countries in Italian? This newspaper headline mentions talks between the USA and the Soviet Union. Although **gli Stati Uniti** is the Italian for the United States, you will often see the English abbreviation USA used in Italian newspapers.

Conclusi i colloqui Usa-Urss

La Spagna prolunga l'anno scolastico

■ What is different from English about the way the abbreviations are written?
■ What is different about the abbreviation for the Soviet Union? Look it up in an Italian-English dictionary.

Delegazione della Cina seleziona film italiani

Gli emigranti

Over the hundred years from the middle of the 19th century, approximately 12 million people left Italy to work or settle in other countries. Early 19th-century emigration was to nearby countries, like France, Switzerland and Tunisia. Then emigrants began to travel further to the Americas in search of a new life. During the 1860s and 1870s, skilled workers from northern Italy crossed the Atlantic. From 1880 on, there was mass emigration from the south of Italy.

Half of all Italian emigrants went to the United States. A quarter went to Argentina and more than a million to Brazil. Another million went to Canada and Australia.

Since World War II, improved economic conditions have reduced the number of permanent emigrants from Italy. However, large numbers of Italians still spend some time working abroad in Switzerland, West Germany, France or Britain.

LODI

Comune del Parco Adda Sud

gemellato con

LODI CALIFORNIA (USA)
COSTANZA (D)
OMEGNA (I)

In lower Manhattan, New York, is a neighborhood called Little Italy. It took on its Italian atmosphere at the end of the 19th century, as emigration from Italy reached its peak in the 1890s.

On Mulberry Street in Little Italy, there is a San Gennaro festival every September. Stands in the street sell Italian food specialities.

Lodi, **un comune** in **Lombardia**, is an agricultural town. It is an important dairy farming center. Its American twin town, Lodi, in California, is a wine-producing area, which has an annual wine festival.
■ What is the name of the other Italian town Lodi is twinned with?

The Food and Agriculture Organization (FAO) is an agency of the United Nations. Set up in 1945, it aims to combat world hunger by raising food production and nutrition levels in developing countries. FAO programs include financial and technical assistance for reforestation, prevention of soil erosion, and general improvement of farming techniques. There is a system for gathering and analyzing information on crop failures and pest invasions throughout the world, so assistance can be given quickly where needed.

Roma was chosen for the FAO headquarters, because King **Vittorio Emanuele III** was the only head of state who would sponsor such an organization at the time.

Answers

7: Poco nuvoloso = not very cloudy; snow and fog in the Alps; arrows show wind force and direction; rain in northern Italy and Sardinia. **8:** Nuclear-free commune.

11: Pietro is Italian and from Turin. He doesn't speak English. **Maria Santorini** is Italian and from Messina in Sicily. She speaks a little English.

15: Roman road = **strada romana**.

18: 900th anniversary.

21: Australia and Antarctica not represented because they had not been discovered.

23: Dante (see p. 4 & 76); Mazzini (see p. 22); **Colombo** (Columbus) discovered the Americas (See p. 79).

25: 2 bedrooms; no separate dining room; only one bathroom. **C** is advertisement for apartment.

26: Chianti. **27:** Her grandparents.

30: 6,000 & 6,500 lire; **blocchetto** ticket is one of a set of 10; 2 journeys have been used.

31: Ticket to Venice is 2nd class; ticket via Vicenza starts in Padua. Rome train leaves from platform 4. **Alitalia (all'Italia)** = to Italy.

32: No lunch after 2 p.m. Sea view. 3-star hotel; low season is 5/20–7/11 and 9/6–10/10; 5,000 lire per day extra; service and tax included; yes. **33:** Yes, near sea; **alberato** = tree-lined; **bambinopoli**; 12,000 lire in high season.

34: 22,000 people an hour. **35:** Chair lift; 8:30 & 11 a.m./6 & 7 p.m. Sledges. Chair lift; 12:30–2:30 p.m.

36: Glass. Hiking, mountain climbing, horseback riding, tennis & fishing; cinema, games room, disco & shopping. **Non accendete fuochi nei boschi**; don't damage flowers and trees. **37:** Protected zone. Beware of the dog.

39: 1,525 hotels, 40,720 rooms. Roads 110 km/h, motorways 140 km/h. Milan-Rome 553 km. Restaurant, telephone, breakdown service.

40: 12 apartments; yes, parking space; **angolo cottura**; living room, bedrooms, bathroom (with shower), corner kitchen, balcony or garden with sea view; includes all; 700,000 lire. **41:** With her family; in Cefalù Sicily.

43: Eat me. The Pantheon. To Trastevere — **Prenda il viale delle Mura Aurelie. Sempre dritto e prenda la prima a sinistra**. To the Pantheon — **Attraversi la Piazza Venezia. Prenda la via del Corso. Giri a sinistra.**

44: St. Callisto & St. Sebastiano. **50:** 1,500, 1,800 & 2,000; **da** asportare.

54: Sono le sei e cinque.

55: Ercolano & Pompei.

56: 30 mins to Naples.

59: No. 20190.

60: Antipasto F, primo B, secondo E, contorno A & D, dolce C. Skiers; drinks. **Caciotta** cheese made with cow's milk.

62: Fish. 12,000 lire; only one **contorno**; no dessert; no wine.

63: Coffee and chocolate with cream; iced tea and coffee.

64: In Italian should be spelled **chilo. 65:** Bread. Horse meat, household equipment. **Mattino & pomeriggio.** Closed Saturday afternoon.

67: 15% discount.

68: 700 lire. **Per tutte le altre destinazioni** (right). **Nord, sud, est, ovest. 69:** 100 & 200 lire coins. 10,000 lire.

70: Dove is symbol of peace.

72: 15–24 group think AC Milan will win; by profession; students and housewives think AC Milan will win. **73: Campionato mondiale.**

74: The Last Emperor. It's an Italian-made western; flash; 17.55 **Oggi al Parlamento**; weather at 11.55. **75:** Sport. Luca Carboni & Terence Trent D'Arby.

76: History of Rome.

79: Omegna.

Acknowledgements

Agenzia Viking, Rimini; Albins; Azienda Riviera del Conero Ancona; Baseball Club Novara; Caremar, Naples; Centrovacanze, Pinzolo (TR); De Stijl Incentive S.A.S.; Donadio; Don Diego Camping, Grottamare; Italian State Tourist Offices in Ancona, Genoa, London, Novara, Rimini, Trento; Turin, Ferrovie dello Stato; Hotel Lago di Braies, Braies (BO); Hotel Promotions Services Ltd., London; La Gazzetta dello Sport; La Stampa; Macelleria Carlin; Museo dell'Automobile Carlo Biscaretti di Ruffia, Turin; Navigazione Lago di Como; Parma Angels Baseball; Polenghi Italia/Fedital SpA; Produttori del Barbaresco, Barbaresco; Residence Gigli, Ancona; Riky Hotel, Bardonecchia; Tourisport Bardonecchia; Ufficio Turistico Pro Loco, Monteresso al mare; Vogue Italia;